CUET

(UG) & Integrated PG

2022

Political Science

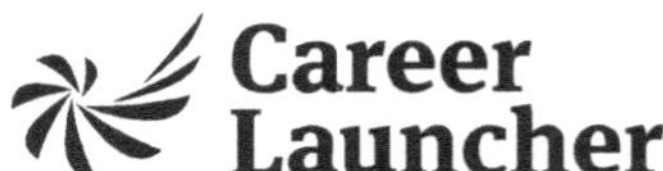

Career
Launcher

Title : CUET 2022 : Political Science

Language : English

Editor's Name : Pravin Choubey, Aparna Aman

Copyright © : 2022 CLIP

Typeset & Published by :

Career Launcher Infrastructure (P) Ltd.

A-45, Mohan Cooperative Industrial Area, Near Mohan Estate Metro Station, New Delhi - 110044

Marketed by :

G.K. Publications (P) Ltd.

Plot No. 9A, Sector-27A, Mathura Road, Faridabad, Haryana-121003

ISBN : 978-93-95101-24-0

Printer's Details : Printed in India, New Delhi.

For product information :

Visit ***www.gkpublications.com*** or email to ***gkp@gkpublications.com***

CONTENTS

About CUET

A year ago, it would have been unimaginable that cut-offs in Delhi University would skyrocket to 100% for some of the undergraduate courses! While DU has always been known for its high cut-offs, there are several other universities where the story is no different.

However, the National Education Policy 2020 (NEP) aims to do away with the tyranny of the ever-rising cut-offs by introducing a Common Entrance Test for all the Central Universities in the country. NEP not only proposes a holistic approach in evaluating the students by giving them the option to select subjects based on their interest, but it also aims to simplify the process of admission to higher-education institutes.

To start with, there would be a Common Entrance Test for all the Central Universities, which would be conducted twice a year from 2022. While this might sound like a new concept to many, the fact is, there is already a CUET, which is conducted for the Central Universities established in or after 2009. As many as 14 of them already admit students based on their performance in the entrance test. The CUET scores are also accepted by four state universities of the country.

The proposed CUET aims to assess conceptual understanding and application of knowledge; and also, to lessen the burden of appearing in multiple tests.

CUET Eligibility

Getting into a premier University is every student's dream. The brand value of the University not only facilitates securing a seat in a master's program in a national/international institute, but also helps in getting job offers through campus placements.

Entry to a Central University, in most cases earlier, was based on merit, i.e., marks secured in Class XII Board exams. However, from the academic year 2021, all Central Universities will also consider the CUET score for admissions into their Undergraduate programs.

CUET 2022: Eligibility Criteria

While the official criteria will be learnt once the CUET 2021 notification is released, the stipulations are not expected to change much from those of previous years.

- A candidate must have passed Class XII (10+2) or equivalent from a recognized education Board.
- If the respective Board awards grades (or CGPA), the conversion factor given by the Board must be used to compute the percentage of marks.
- Candidates, who have completed their Class XII in 2021, and have passed the Board exams, will also be eligible to apply for CUET 2022.

Eligibility: Class XII Students

While CUET is for students who have passed the Class XII (or equivalent) Board exams, any student who is appearing for the Class XII Board exam in 2022 is also eligible to apply for CUET 2021. The candidate would be required to produce the marksheets and relevant certificates as mandated by the participating Central University, and follow the timelines provided for admissions.

Key Points

- Each participating Central University is free to decide its own eligibility criteria for admissions.

- The weightages for CUET and Class XII Board exam results(if applicable) will be at the sole discretion of the Central University, to which admission is being sought.

- As of date, CUET does not have an age limit. However, Central Universities can fix minimum & maximum age limit for admissions to all (or any) of the programs on offer.

Reservation of Seats

As CUET is an entrance exam for admissions to Undergraduate courses at the Central Universities, which have been established under an Act of the Parliament, each Central University must follow the norms set by the Government of India, with respect to intake and reservation of seats.

Generally, the following break-up is followed:

Category	Reservation
Scheduled Castes	15%
Scheduled Tribes	7.5%
Other Backward Classes (Non-Creamy)	27%
Persons with Disability	5%

Some institutions might even have provisions for the Economically Weaker Sections, which can account for 10% of the total seats. These EWS seats are carved out from the Open Category.

To avail of the reservation benefit based on caste (or any other category as specified), a candidate must be able to produce valid documents/certificates to support such claims.

Conclusion

It is essential for every candidate to check the validity of their candidature for CUET, as well as the Central University he/she is applying to. The candidate should be aware of the documents that might be required while applying for the exam, or during the admissions.

CUET 2022 notification is expected in March 2022, and registration is also going to start then.

CUET: Exam Pattern

Examination Structure for CUET (UG) -2022:

CUET (UG) –2022 will consist of the following 4 Sections:

    Section IA –13 Languages
    Section IB –19 Languages
    Section II –27 Domain specific Subjects
    Section III –General Test

Choosing options from each Section is not mandatory. Choices should match the requirements of the desired University.

Broad features of CUET (UG) -2022 are as follows:

Section	Subjects/ Tests	Questions to be Attempted	Question Type	Duration
Section IA – Languages	There are 13* different languages. Any of these languages may be chosen.	40 questions to be attempted out of 50 in each language	Language to be tested through Reading Comprehension (based on different types of passages–Factual, Literary and Narrative, [Literary Aptitude and Vocabulary]	45 Minutes for each language
Section IB – Languages	There are 19** Languages. Any other language apart from those offered in Section I A may be chosen.			
Section II - Domain	There are 27*** Domains specific subjects being offered under this Section. A candidate may choose a maximum of Six (06) Domains as desired by the applicable University/Universities.	40 Questions to be attempted out of 50	• Input text can be used for MCQ Based Questions • MCQs based on NCERT Class XII syllabus only	
Section III- General Test	For any such undergraduate programme/ programmes being offered by Universities where a General Test is being used for admission.	60 Questions to be attempted out of 75	• Input text can be used for MCQ Based Questions • General Knowledge, Current Affairs, General Mental Ability, Numerical Ability, Quantitative Reasoning (Simple application of basic mathematical concepts arithmetic/algebra geometry/mensuration/s tat taught till Grade 8), Logical and Analytical Reasoning	

* **Languages (13):** Tamil, Telugu, Kannada, Malayalam, Marathi, Gujarati, Odiya, Bengali, Assamese, Punjabi, English, Hindi and Urdu

** **Languages (19):** *French, Spanish, German, Nepali, Persian, Italian, Arabic, Sindhi, Kashmiri, Konkani, Bodo, Dogri, Maithili, Manipuri, Santhali, Tibetan, Japanese, Russian, Chinese.*

*** **Domain Specific Subjects (27):** 1. Accountancy/ Book Keeping 2. Biology/ Biological Studies/ Biotechnology/Biochemistry 3. Business Studies 4. Chemistry 5. Computer Science/ Informatics Practices 6. Economics/ Business Economics 7. Engineering Graphics 8.Entrepreneurship 9. Geography/Geology 10. History 11. Home Science 12.Knowledge Tradition and Practices of India 13. Legal Studies 14. Environmental Science 15. Mathematics 16. Physical Education/ NCC /Yoga 17.Physics 18.Political Science 19. Psychology 20. Sociology 21. Teaching Aptitude 22. Agriculture 23. Mass Media/ Mass Communication 24. Anthropology 25. Fine Arts/Visual Arts (Sculpture/ Painting)/Commercial Arts, 26. Performing Arts – (i) Dance (Kathak/ Bharatnatyam/Oddisi/ Kathakali/Kuchipudi/ Manipuri (ii) Drama- Theatre (iii) Music General (Hindustani/ Carnatic/ RabindraSangeet/ Percussion/ Non-Percussion), 27. Sanskrit *[For all Shastri (Shastri 3 years/ 4 years Honours) Equivalent to B.A./B.A. Honours courses i.e. Shastri in Veda, Paurohitya (Karmakand), Dharamshastra, Prachin Vyakarana, Navya Vyakarana, Phalit Jyotish, Siddhant Jyotish, Vastushastra, Sahitya,Puranetihas, Prakrit Bhasha,Prachin Nyaya Vaisheshik, Sankhya Yoga, Jain Darshan, Mimansa, AdvaitaVedanta, Vishihstadvaita Vedanta, Sarva Darshan, a candidate may choose Sanskrit as the Domain].*

- A Candidate can choose a maximum of **any 3 languages** from Section IA and Section IB taken together. (One of the languages chosen needs to be in lieu of Domain specific subjects)
- Section II offers 27 Subjects, out of which a candidate may choose a **maximum of 6 Subjects**.
- Section III comprises **General Test.**
- For choosing Languages (upto 3) from Section IA and IB and a maximum of 6 Subjects from Section II and General Test under Section III, the Candidate must refer to the requirements of his/her intended University.

Mode of the Test	Computer Based Test-CBT
Test Pattern	Objective type with Multiple Choice Questions
Medium	13 languages (*Tamil, Telugu, Kannada, Malayalam, Marathi, Gujarati, Odiya, Bengali, Assamese, Punjabi, English, Hindi and Urdu*)
Syllabus	**Section IA & IB:** Language to be tested through Reading Comprehension (based on different types of passages–Factual, Literary and Narrative [Literary Aptitude & Vocabulary]
	Section II : As per NCERT model syllabus as applicable to Class XII only
	Section III : General Knowledge, Current Affairs, General Mental Ability, Numerical Ability, Quantitative Reasoning (Simple application of basic mathematical concepts arithmetic/algebra geometry/mensuration/stat taught till Grade 8), Logical and Analytical Reasoning

Level of questions for CUET (UG) -2022:

All questions in various testing areas will be benchmarked at the level of Class XII only. Students having studied Class XII Board syllabus would be able to do well in CUET (UG) – 2022.

Number of attempts:

If any University permits students of previous years of class XII to take admission in the current year also, such students would also be eligible to appear in CUET (UG) – 2022.

Choice of Languages and Subjects:

Generally the languages/subjects chosen should be the ones that a student has opted in his latest Class XII Board examination. However, if any University permits any flexibility in this regards, the same can be exercised under CUET (UG) -2022 also. Candidates must carefully refer to the eligibility requirements of various Central Universities in this regard. Moreover, if the subject to be studied in the Undergraduate course is not available in the list of **27 Domain Specific Subject** being offered, the Candidate may choose the Subject closest to his choice for e.g. For Biochemistry the candidate may choose Biology.

Candidates are advised to visit the NTA CUET (UG)-2022 official website **https://cuet.samarth.ac.in/** for latest updates regarding the Examination.

CUET Syllabus

CUET Syllabus

Before you start your preparation for any entrance exam, it is important to understand the syllabus. Otherwise, your prep will be directionless, and you might be left wondering where things might have gone wrong!

With more than 1.68 lakh seats on offer for the undergraduate courses at the 54 Central Universities, CUET is one the most competitive examinations. For this very reason, while preparing for the exam, you will need to adopt a structured approach. And in doing that, understanding the syllabus is a critical step.

CUET 2022 Overview

CUET 2022 will be a Computer-Based Test (CBT), commonly referred to as an online exam. However, there is a difference between the two terms: CBT and online. In CBT, the questions are kept constant and simply presented in an online format; whereas in an Online Test, questions are stored as a bank, and the system decides which questions are to be presented to the candidate, based on a pre-defined logic.

CUET 2022 is likely to be a General Ability Test, with focus on English Language, Numerical Ability, Logical & Analytical Reasoning, along with General Awareness and Current Affairs.

CUET 2022 Syllabus

The CUET 2022 exam pattern gives a good idea about what is in store for the candidate and how one needs to prepare for the exam.

- **English Language:** The questions in this section will test one's proficiency in the language, based on comprehension passages, fundamentals of grammar, and vocabulary. In the Comprehension section, candidates will be evaluated on their understanding of a passage and its central theme, meanings of words used therein, etc. The Grammar section entails correcting grammatically incorrect sentences, filling of blanks in sentences with appropriate words, etc. Questions on synonyms & antonyms will check one's command over English vocabulary.
- **Numerical Ability:** Questions on Numerical Ability will test the candidate's knowledge of elementary mathematics. Areas like arithmetic, number system, basics of algebra, and modern maths will be central to these types of questions.
- **Logical & Analytical Reasoning:** This section tests the candidate's ability to identify patterns & logical links, and rectify illogical arguments. It can include a variety of Logical Reasoning questions, such as those on syllogisms, logical sequences, analogies, etc., along with Analytical Reasoning questions on series, directions, clocks & calendars, arrangements, and puzzles to name a few.
- **General Awareness and Current Affairs:** The General Awareness section includes static general knowledge, while questions on Current Affairs will gauge a candidate's knowledge of national & international current affairs.

CUET 2022 may or may not have a section on subject knowledge. Once the exam notification is out in March, there will be more clarity on this matter.

While there is no syllabus explicitly mentioned by CUET, the broad idea is always presented. One must look at the previous years' papers and solve the sample papers available to form a basic understanding.

About University of Delhi

University of Delhi (commonly known as DU) was established in 1922 and is one of the largest Universities in the country. With 16 faculties, 86 academic departments, 90 colleges and 540 programs on offer, Delhi University is no doubt one of the sought-after University in the country.

With 1, 96,000 students enrolled in UG programs, Delhi University is a valued university and constantly ranked among the top in the country. DU bagged 11th Rank in NIRF 2020 and ranked 6th in QS India Rankings 2020. The University has two Campuses: North and South.

DU UG Programs

Delhi University offers several programs at the undergraduate level. With more than 60 constituent colleges, the Delhi University offers many undergraduate courses.

Please refer to the table below for the important undergraduate courses offered by the DU and the intake across each program.

Program	Intake
B. A (Pass)	11249
B. A (Hons) Geography	788
B. A (Hons) Economics	2754
B. A (Hons) History	2791
B. A (Hons) Political Science	3657
B. A (Hons) Sociology	596
B. A (Hons) Psychology	670
B. A (Hons) Applied Psychology	252
B. A (Hons) Social Work	133
B. A (Hons) Philosophy	783
B. A (Hons) English	2886
B. A (Hons) Hindi	2829
B. A (Hons) Sanskrit	1407
B. A (Hons) Punjabi	214
B. A (Hons) Urdu	207
BA(Hons) French	49

Program	Intake
BA(Hons) German	49
BA(Hons) Spanish	49
BA(Hons) Italian	49
B. Com (Hons)	7953
B.Com (Pass)	7854
Program	Intake
B.Sc. (H) Biomedical Science	162
B.Sc. (H) Botany	937
B.Sc. (H) Chemistry	1487
B.Sc. (H) Computer Science	1265
B.Sc. (H) Electronics	624
B.Sc. (H) Mathematics	2428
B.Sc. (H) Physics	1659
B.Sc. (H) Zoology	944
B.Sc. Life Sciences	1515
B.Sc. Physical Science with Chemistry	703
B.Sc. Physical Science with Computer Science	553
B.Sc. Physical Science with Electronics	247
B. Sc (Hons.) Statistics	476
B. Sc. (Prog.) Applied Physical Science Industrial Chemistry	96
B.Sc. (Hons.) Home Science	900
B. Sc. (Hons.) Psychology	57
B.Sc. (H) Food Technology	179
B.Sc. (H)Instrumentation	99
B.Sc. (H) Microbiology	238
B.Sc. (H) Polymer Science	59
B.SC. Mathematical Science	224
B.SC. (Hons.) Biochemistry	146
B.SC. Industrial Chemistry	78
B.Sc. (Prog.) Physical Science	940
B.SC. (Hons.) Geology	98

DU UG Programs Eligibility:

As the University offers multiple programs and separate intake for male and female candidates, it is important to check the university official website regularly to keep oneself updated about the eligibility for each program, which can change.

DU UG Admissions:

Until 2021, Delhi University admitted students on the basis of class XII marks. From the academic year 2022, admissions to UG programs offered Delhi University will be based on CUET. CUET will be a common entrance for admissions to UG programs offered by all the Central Universities in the country.

Delhi University UG Programs Reservation:

DU being a Central University offers reservations in admissions according to central government rules.

Schedule Caste (SC): 15% of the total seats are reserved for students who belong to SC category.

Schedule Tribe (ST): 7.5% of the total seats are reserved for students belonging to ST Category.

Other Backward Classes (OBC): 27% of the total intake is reserved for students from Other Backward Classes (OBC), excluding those from creamy layer.

Economically Weaker Section (EWS): The University has reserved 10% seats for EWS category, in accordance with the directive of Ministry of Education.

Persons with Disability (PWD): 5% of the seats are reserved on horizontal basis for students from PWD category.

About BHU

Banaras Hindu University (BHU), situated in the holy city of Varanasi, was founded by Pandit Madan Mohan Malviya in cooperation with Dr. Annie Besant, in 1916 under the act of Parliament-B.H.U Act, 1915. BHU, which is a Central University, comprises of 6 Institutes, 14 Faculties, 144 academic departments, and 4 Inter-disciplinary centers, spread over 1300 acres. The University consists of 15,000 students, 1700 teachers and 8000 non-teaching staff.

BHU was ranked 3rd among the Universities in India in 2020. According to university submissions for NIRF 2021, BHU has 10, 585 students pursuing UG programs, of which 236 students are foreign nationals.

BHU UG Programs

BHU offers a host of undergraduate programs including medical and engineering. Through its various faculties, BHU offers a range of programs which caters to students learning abilities. The University along with its main campus, also offers the undergraduate courses from the following colleges: Mahila Mahavidyalaya (MMV); Arya Mahila Post Graduate College (AMPGC), Vasant Kanya Mahavidyalaya (VKM); Vasanta College for Women (VCW); DAV Post Graduate College (DAVPGC) and Rajiv Gandhi South Campus (RGSC).

Please refer to the table below for the important undergraduate courses offered by BHU and the intake across each program/campuses.

Faculty of Arts				
Course	Campus	Intake	Status	Duration
B.A (Hons) Arts	Faculty of Arts	765	Co-Ed	3 Years
	Mahila Mahavidyalaya	286	Women	3 Years
	Arya Mahila Post Graduate College	383	Women	3 Years
	Vasant Kanya Mahavidyalaya	286	Women	3 Years
	Vasanta College for Women	412	Women	3 Years
	DAV Post Graduate College	309	Co-Ed	3 Years
Faculty of Social Sciences				
Course	Campus	Intake	Status	Duration
B.A (Hons) Social Sciences [incl. B. A (Hons) Economics]	Faculty of Social Sciences	573	Co-Ed	3 Years
	Mahila Mahavidyalaya	193	Women	3 Years
	Arya Mahila Post Graduate College	383	Women	3 Years
	Vasant Kanya Mahavidyalaya	249	Women	3 Years
	Vasanta College for Women	210	Women	3 Years
	DAV Post Graduate College	326	Co-Ed	3 Years

Faculty of Commerce				
Course	Campus	Intake	Status	Duration
B. Com (Hons)	Faculty of Commerce	286	Co-Ed	3 Years
	Vasant Kanya Mahavidyalaya	96	Women	3 Years
	Arya Mahila Post Graduate College	96	Women	3 Years
	DAV Post Graduate College	227	Co-Ed	3 Years
	Rajiv Gandhi South Campus, Mirzapur	114	Co-Ed	3 Years
B. Com (Hons) Financial Markets Management	Faculty of Commerce	62	Co-Ed	3 Years
	Rajiv Gandhi South Campus, Mirzapur	62	Co-Ed	3 Years

Institute of Science				
Course	Campus	Intake	Status	Duration
B.Sc (Hons) Maths Group	Faculty of Science	573	Co-Ed	3 Years
	Mahila Mahavidyalaya	96	Women	3 Years
B.Sc (Hons) Bio Group	Faculty of Science	383	Co-Ed	3 Years
	Mahila Mahavidyalaya	193	Women	3 Years

Faculty of Visual Arts				
Course	Campus	Intake	Status	Duration
B.F.A (Bachelor of Fine Arts)	Faculty of Visual Arts	96	Co-Ed	4 Years
Faculty of Arts				
Bachelor of Vocation (Retail and Logistics Management)	Rajiv Gandhi South Campus	62	Co-Ed	3 Years
Bachelor of Vocation (Hospitality & Tourism Management)	Rajiv Gandhi South Campus	62	Co-Ed	3 Years
Bachelor of Vocation (Fashion Designing and Event Management)	Rajiv Gandhi South Campus	62	Co-Ed	3 Years
Bachelor of Vocation (Modern Office Management)	Rajiv Gandhi South Campus	62	Co-Ed	3 Years
Bachelor of Vocation (Food Processing & Management)	Rajiv Gandhi South Campus	62	Co-Ed	3 Years
Bachelor of Vocation (Medical Lab. & Technology)	Rajiv Gandhi South Campus	62	Co-Ed	3 Years

BHU UG Programs Eligibility:

Each of the courses have different eligibility for admissions. To be eligible for admissions, one must fulfil all the criteria as laid down by the respective faculties of the University.

B.A (Hons) Arts/ B.A (Hons) Social Sciences: Candidate must not be more than 22 years of age and must have passed class XII or equivalent with minimum 50% marks in aggregate.

B.A (Hons) Economics: Candidate must not be more than 22 years of age and must have passed class XII or equivalent with minimum 50% marks in aggregate along with mathematics as one of the papers.

B. Com (Hons)/B. Com (Hons) Financial Markets Management: Candidate must not be more than 22 years of age and must have passed class XII or equivalent with minimum 50% marks in aggregate with Commerce/ Economics/Maths/Computer Science/Finance/Financial Markets Management as one of the subjects.

B. Sc (Hons) Maths Group: Candidate must not be more than 22 years of age and must have passed class XII or equivalent with minimum 50% marks in aggregate in the subjects Physics, Maths plus any one of the following: Chemistry, Statistics, Geology, Computer Science, Information Technology and Geography and must have passed in each of the concerned three subjects.

B. Sc (Hons) Bio Group: Candidate must not be more than 22 years of age and must have passed class XII or equivalent with minimum 50% marks in aggregate in the subjects Physics, Chemistry plus any one of the following: Biology, Geology and Geography and must have passed in each of the concerned three subjects.

B. F. A (Bachelor of Fine Arts): Candidate must not be more than 22 years of age and must have passed class XII or equivalent with minimum 50% marks in aggregate.

Bachelor of Vocation: Candidate must have passed class XII or equivalent in any stream (Science for Food Processing and Medical Lab Technology) or level 4 NSQF certificate.

BHU UG Admissions:

Until 2021, admissions to BHU UG courses were based on Undergraduate Entrance Test (UET) conducted by the University. From the academic year 2022, admissions to UG programs offered by BHU will be based on CUET, which will replace the UET. CUET will be a common entrance for admissions to UG programs offered by all the Central Universities in the country.

BHU UG Programs Reservation:

BHU being a Central University offers reservations in admissions according to central government rules.

Schedule Caste (SC): 15% of the total seats are reserved for students who belong to SC category.

Schedule Tribe (ST): 7.5% of the total seats are reserved for students belonging to ST Category.

Other Backward Classes (OBC): 27% of the total intake is reserved for students from Other Backward Classes (OBC), excluding those from creamy layer.

Economically Weaker Section (EWS): The University has reserved 10% seats for EWS category, in accordance with the directive of Ministry of Education.

Persons with Disability (PWD): 5% of the seats are reserved on horizontal basis for students from PWD category.

About JNU

Ever wondered which University, the cadets from National Defence Academy (NDA) graduate from? Yes. It is Jawaharlal Nehru University (JNU). JNU started in the year 1969, three years after the act of Parliament in 1966. With several academic centres of JNU declared "Centres of Excellence" by the University Grants Commission, JNU has been ranked No. 1 by National Assessment and Accreditation Council (NAAC). JNU has been ranked No. 2 by National Institutional Ranking Framework (NIRF) 2020 and has been awarded the Best University Award by the President of India in 2017. The European Commission has awarded the Jean Monnet Centre of Excellence for European Union Studies in India (CEEUSI) to Jawaharlal Nehru University in 2018. This is one of the highest international recognition for any European Studies programme.

JNU was the first University to start integrated five-year Master of Arts in Language Courses. JNU actively collaborates with National and International Universities for student and faculty exchange programs.

According to university submissions for NIRF 2020, JNU has 1,048 students pursuing UG programs, of which 46 are foreign nationals.

JNU UG Programs

JNU offers a limited program at the undergraduate level, unlike other universities. The focus at undergraduate has been largely on language courses. In 2018, JNU started two programs in engineering and plans to add a few more specializations in future.

Please refer to the table below for the important undergraduate courses offered by JNU and the intake across each program.

School	Program	Intake	Duration
School of Language, Literature and Cultural Studies	B. A (Hons) Pashto	19	3 Years
	B. A (Hons) Persian	39	3 Years
	B. A (Hons) Arabic	39	3 Years
	B. A (Hons) Japanese	48	3 Years
	B. A (Hons) Korean	39	3 Years
	B. A (Hons) Chinese	44	3 Years
	B. A (Hons) French	48	3 Years
	B. A (Hons) German	48	3 Years
	B. A (Hons) Russian	68	3 Years
	B. A (Hons) Spanish	39	3 Years

School of Sanskrit and Indic Studies	B. Sc - M. Sc Integrated Program in Ayurveda Biology	20	5 Years
School of Engineering	B. Tech in Computer Science and Engineering & MS/M. Tech in Social Sciences/Humanities/Science/Technology	25	5 Years
	B. Tech in Electronics and Communication Engineering & MS/M. Tech in Social Sciences/Humanities/Science/Technology	25	5 Years

JNU UG Programs Eligibility:

Each of the courses have different eligibility for admissions. To be eligible for admissions, one must fulfil all the criteria as laid down by the respective faculties of the University.

B.A (Hons) Language Courses: Candidate must not be less than 17 years of age and must have passed Senior School Certificate (10+2) or equivalent examination with minimum of 45% marks.

B. Sc - M. Sc Integrated Program in Ayurveda Biology: Candidate must not be less than 17 years of age and must have passed Senior School Certificate (10+2) or equivalent examination with minimum of 45% marks.

B. Tech-M. Tech: Based on JEE Mains

JNU UG Admissions:

Until 2021, admissions to JNU UG courses were based on JNU Entrance Examination (JNUEE) conducted by the National Testing Agency (NTA). From the academic year 2022, admissions to UG programs offered by JNU will be based on CUET, which will replace the JNUEE. CUET will be a common entrance for admissions to UG programs offered by all the Central Universities in the country.

JNU UG Programs Reservation:

JNU being a Central University offers reservations in admissions according to central government rules.

Schedule Caste (SC): 15% of the total seats are reserved for students who belong to SC category.

Schedule Tribe (ST): 7.5% of the total seats are reserved for students belonging to ST Category.

Other Backward Classes (OBC): 27% of the total intake is reserved for students from Other Backward Classes (OBC), excluding those from creamy layer. Also, Central List of Caste to be followed.

Economically Weaker Section (EWS): The University has reserved 10% seats for EWS category, in accordance with the directive of Ministry of Education.

Persons with Disability (PWD): 5% of the seats are reserved on horizontal basis for students from PWD category.

About Jamia Milia Islamia

Jamia Milia Islamia (JMI) was founded in 1920 in Aligarh and became a Central University in 1988 by the act of Parliament. Jamia in Urdu stands for University and Milia means National, making Jamia Milia Islamia a National University. Jamia Milia Islamia moved to Delhi in 1925 and shifted to its present campus in Okhla in 1935.

Jamia Milia Islamia is a NAAC accredited University with grade "A" and was placed 10th in NIRF Rankings 2020. According to submissions made by University for NIRF 2021, Jamia Milia Islamia has a total of 5,911 students pursuing undergraduate courses at the University, of which 105 are foreign nationals. The University also manage to place a total of 681 UG students with an average salary ranging 4.2 Lacs-6.0 Lacs.

JMI UG Programs

Jamia Milia Islamia (JMI) offers a host of undergraduate programs for students. Through its various faculties, JMI offers a range of programs which caters to students learning abilities.

Please refer to the table below for the important undergraduate courses offered by Jamia Milia Islamia and the intake across each program.

Faculty	Course	Intake	Duration
Faculty of Humanities and Language	B. A (Hons) English	60	3 Years
	B. A (Hons) Hindi	40	3 Years
	B. A (Hons) Mass Media-Hindi	40	3 Years
	B. A (Hons) History	60	3 Years
	Bachelor of Hotel Management (BHM)	40	3 Years
	Bachelor of Tourism and Travel Management	40	3 Years
	B. Voc (Food Production)	40	3 Years
Faculty of Social Sciences	Bachelor of Arts (B. A)	68	3 Years
	B. Com (Hons)	55	3 Years
	BBA (Bachelor of Business Administration)	44	3 Years
	B. A (Hons) Economics	53	3 Years
	B. A (Hons) Sociology	42	3 Years
	B. A (Hons) Political Science	42	3 Years
	B. A (Hons) Psychology	42	3 Years
Faculty of Natural Sciences	B. Sc (Bachelor of Science)	50	3 Years
	B. Sc Biosciences	40	3 Years
	B. Sc Biotechnology	35	3 Years
	B. Sc (Hons) Chemistry	40	3 Years
	B. A/B. Sc (Hons) Geography	60	3 Years
	B. Sc (Hons) Mathematics	45	3 Years
	B. Sc (Hons) Applied Mathematics	45	3 Years
	B. Sc (Hons) Physics	45	3 Years
Faculty of Fine Arts	Bachelor of Fine Arts (Applied Art)	30	4 Years
	Bachelor of Fine Arts (Art Education)	20	4 Years
	Bachelor of Fine Arts (Painting)	20	4 Years
	Bachelor of Fine Arts (Sculpture)	10	4 Years

JMI UG Programs Eligibility:

Each of the courses have different eligibility for admissions. To be eligible for admissions, one must fulfil all the criteria as laid down by the respective faculties of the University.

B. Com (Hons) /BBA /B. A (Hons) Economics: Candidate must have passed class XII or equivalent with a minimum of 50% marks in five subjects.

BHM/BTTM/B. Voc (Food Production): Candidate must have passed class XII or equivalent with a minimum of 45% marks in five subjects.

B. A (Hons) Mass Media/B. A (Hons) Hindi: Candidate must have passed class XII or equivalent with a minimum of 45% marks in five subjects.

B. Sc/B. Sc (Hons): Candidate must have passed class XII or equivalent with minimum 50% marks in each of the science subjects i.e. Physics, Chemistry and Mathematics and 50% marks in aggregate of best 5-subjects.

JMI UG Admissions:

Until 2021, admissions to JMI UG courses were based on Entrance Test (JMI-ET) conducted by the University. From the academic year 2022, admissions to UG programs offered by JMI will be based on CUET, which will replace the JMI-ET. CUET will be a common entrance for admissions to UG programs offered by all the Central Universities in the country.

JMI UG Programs Reservation:

JMI is a minority reservation-based University and accordingly, seats are reserved for candidates as per the norms laid down by the University.

Muslim Minority: 30% of the total seats are reserved for Muslim applicants; 10% of the total seats are reserved for women applicants who are Muslim; 10% of the total intake is for OBC-NC candidates who are Muslims.

Persons with Disability (PWD): 5% of the seats are reserved for students from PWD category.

Jamia Students: 5% seats in all Undergraduate Programs shall be filled by internal students of Jamia who have passed their qualifying examination of the concerned programme (X or XII) from Jamia Schools as regular students.

In addition, Jamia Milia Islamia has supernumerary seats for Kashmiri Migrants and students from Jammu and Kashmir.

About Aligarh Muslim University

Aligarh Muslim University also referred as AMU was established by Sir Syed Ahmad Khan in 1875. The University started as Muhammadan Anglo-Oriental College and became a University (AMU) in 1920. The university has been ranked 801–1000 in the QS World University Rankings of 2021 and 17 in India by the National Institutional Ranking Framework in 2020.

Aligarh Muslim University is institution of national importance, under the seventh schedule of the Constitution of India.

AMU UG Programs

Aligarh Muslim University offers several programs at the undergraduate level. With 7 constituent colleges, the Aligarh Muslim University offers many undergraduate courses.

Please refer to the table below for the important undergraduate courses offered by the AMU and the intake across each program.

Course	Intake	Duration
B. Sc (Hons) Home Science	30*	3 Years
B.Sc (Hons) Agriculture	40	4 Years
B. A (Hons) Arabic	20+10*	3 Years
B. A (Hons) Communicative English	15+20*	3 Years
B. A (Hons) English	40+35*	3 Years
B. A (Hons) Hindi	40+25*	3 Years
B. A (Hons) Geography	50+20*	3 Years
B. A (Hons) Linguistics	20+25*	3 Years
B. A (Hons) Persian	15+25*	3 Years
B. A (Hons) Philosophy	20+10*	3 Years
B. A (Hons) Quaranic Studies	10+10*	3 Years
B. A (Hons) Sanskrit	15+10*	3 Years
B. A (Hons) Urdu	40+50*	3 Years
Bachelor of Fine Arts	15+15*	3 Years
B. Com (Hons)	180+100*	3 Years
B. Voc Production Technology	50	3 Years
B Voc Polymer and Coating Technology	50	3 Years
B. Voc Fashion Design and Garment Technology	50	3 Years
B. A (Hons) Chinese	20	3 Years
B. A (Hons) French	20	3 Years
B. A (Hons) German	20	3 Years

B. A (Hons) Russian	20	3 Years
B. A (Hons) Spanish	20	3 Years
B. Sc (Hons) Biochemistry	30+30*	3 Years
B. Sc (Hons) Botany	60+40*	3 Years
B. Sc (Hons) Zoology	60+45*	3 Years
B. Sc (Hons) Physics	120+35*	3 Years
B. Sc (Hons) Chemistry	120+65*	3 Years
B. Sc (Hons) Mathematics	120+40*	3 Years
B. Sc (Hons) Geography	45+30*	3 Years
B. Sc (Hons) Geology	100+30*	3 Years
B. Sc (Hons) Statistics	60+30*	3 Years
B. Sc (Hons) Industrial Chemistry	20+10*	3 Years
B. Sc (Hons) Computer Applications	40+20*	3 Years

AMU UG Programs Eligibility:

As the University offers multiple programs and separate intake for male and female candidates, it is important to check the university official website regularly to keep oneself updated about the eligibility for each program, which can change.

AMU UG Admissions:

Until 2021, AMU conducted its own entrance test to admit students for the UG programs. From the academic year 2022, admissions to UG programs offered by Aligarh Muslim University will be based on CUET. CUET will be a common entrance for admissions to UG programs offered by all the Central Universities in the country.

University of Allahabad UG Programs Reservation:

Allahabad University being a Central University offers reservations in admissions according to central government rules. Kindly check the university website for further details.

POLITICAL SCIENCE
PART – I

The Cold War Era

The end of the Cold War is usually seen as the beginning of the contemporary era in world politics.

Cuban Missile Crisis: In April 1961, the leaders of the Union of Soviet Socialist Republics (USSR) were worried that the United States of America (USA) would invade communist-ruled Cuba and overthrow Fidel Castro, the president of the small island nation off the coast of the United States. Cuba was an ally of the Soviet Union and received both diplomatic and financial aid from it. Nikita Khrushchev, the leader of the Soviet Union, decided to convert Cuba into a Russian base. Kennedy ordered American warships to intercept any Soviet ships heading to Cuba as a way of warning the USSR of his seriousness. A clash seemed imminent in what came to be known as the Cuban Missile Crisis. Eventually, to the world's great relief, both sides decided to avoid war. The Soviet ships slowed down and turned back.

The Cold War referred to the competition, the tensions and a series of confrontations between the United States and Soviet Union, backed by their respective allies.

The western alliance, headed by the US, represented the ideology of liberal democracy and capitalism while the eastern alliance, headed by the Soviet Union, was committed to the ideology of socialism and communism.

Cold War: In 1945, the Allied Forces, led by the US, Soviet Union, Britain and France defeated the Axis Powers led by Germany, Italy and Japan, ending the Second World War (1939-1945). The war had involved almost all the major powers of the world and spread out to regions outside Europe including Southeast Asia, China, Burma (now Myanmar) and parts of India's northeast. The end of the Second World War was also the beginning of the Cold War. The world war ended when the United States dropped two atomic bombs on the Japanese cities of Hiroshima and Nagasaki in August 1945, causing Japan to surrender. While the Cold War was an outcome of the emergence of the US and the USSR as two superpowers rival to each other, it was also rooted in the understanding that the destruction caused by the use of atom bombs is too costly for any country to bear.

The Emergence of Two Power Blocs: The alliance systems led by the two superpowers, therefore, threatened to divide the entire world into two camps. This division happened first in Europe. Most countries of Western Europe sided with the US and those of Eastern Europe joined the Soviet camp. That is why these were also called the 'western' and the 'eastern' alliances. The western alliance was formalised into an organisation, the North Atlantic Treaty Organisation (NATO), which came into existence in April 1949. It was an association of twelve states which declared that armed attack on any one of them in Europe or North America would be regarded as an attack on all of them. Each of these states would be obliged to help the other. The eastern alliance, known as the Warsaw Pact, was led by the Soviet Union. It was created in 1955 and its principal function was to counter NATO's forces in Europe. In East and Southeast Asia and in West Asia (Middle East), the United States built an alliance system called - the Southeast Asian Treaty Organisation (SEATO) and the Central Treaty Organisation (CENTO). The Soviet Union and communist China responded by having close relations with regional countries such as North Vietnam, North Korea and Iraq.

The roots of NAM went back to the friendship between three leaders - Yugoslavia's Josip Broz Tito, India's Jawaharlal Nehru, and Egypt's leader Gamal Abdel Nasser - who held a meeting in 1956. Indonesia's Sukarno and Ghana's Kwame Nkrumah strongly supported them. These five leaders came to be known as the five founders of NAM. The first non-aligned summit was held in Belgrade in 1961.

The policy of staying away from alliances should not be considered isolationism or neutrality. Non-alignment is not isolationism since isolationism means remaining aloof from world affairs. Isolationism sums up the foreign policy of the US from the American War of Independence in 1787 up to the beginning of the First World War. In comparison,

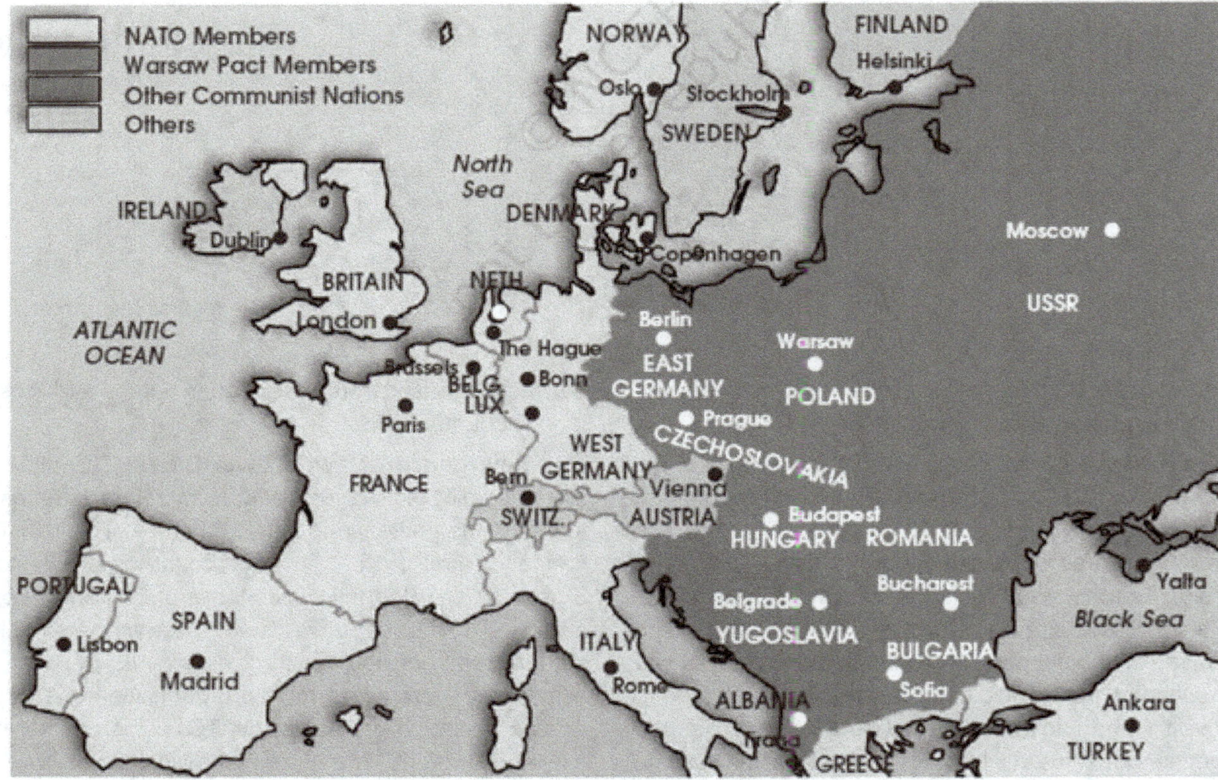

Map showing the way Europe was divided into rival alliances during the Cold War

the non-aligned countries, including India, played an active role in mediating between the two rival alliances in the cause of peace and stability. Their strength was based on their unity and their resolve to remain non-aligned despite the attempt by the two superpowers to bring them into their alliances. Non-alignment is also not neutrality. Neutrality refers principally to a policy of staying out of war. States practicing neutrality are not required to help end a war. They do not get involved in wars and do not take any position on the appropriateness or morality of a war. Non-aligned states, including India, were actually involved in wars for various reasons. They also worked to prevent war between others and tried to end wars that had broken out.

The United Nations Conference on Trade and Development (UNCTAD) brought out a report in 1972 entitled Towards a New Trade Policy for Development. The report proposed a reform of the global trading system so as to:

(i)   give the LDCs control over their natural resources exploited by the developed Western countries,

(ii)   obtain access to Western markets so that the LDCs could sell their products and, therefore, make trade more beneficial for the poorer countries,

(iii)   reduce the cost of technology from the Western countries, and

(iv)   provide the LDCs with a greater role in international economic institutions.

As a leader of NAM, India's response to the ongoing Cold War was two-fold: At one level, it took particular care in staying away from the two alliances. Second, it raised its voice against the newly decolonised countries becoming part of these alliances.

Limited Test Ban Treaty (LTBT): Banned nuclear weapon tests in the atmosphere, in outer space and under water. Signed by the US, UK and USSR in Moscow on 5 August 1963. Entered into force on 10 October 1963.

Nuclear Non-proliferation Treaty (NPT): Allows only the nuclear weapon states to have nuclear weapons and stops others from acquiring them. For the purposes of the NPT, a nuclear weapon state is one which has manufactured and exploded a nuclear weapon or other nuclear explosive device prior to 1 January 1967. So there are five nuclear weapon states: US, USSR (later Russia), Britain, France and China. Signed in Washington, London, and Moscow on 1 July 1968. Entered into force on 5 March 1970. Extended indefinitely in 1995.

Exercise

Level – 1

1. At the end of cold war era, which of the following era of world politics began?

(a) Modern

(b) Middle

(c) Upper

(d) Contemporary

2. Which of the following order is established by the non-aligned countries?

(a) New International Economic Order

(b) New International Social Order

(c) New International Political Order

(d) New International Power Order

3. The Battle of Iwo Jima was fought in which year?

(a) 1939   (b) 1945

(c) 1940   (d) 1941

4. Who was the President of Cuba during Cuban Missile Crisis?

(a) Fidel Castro

(b) Nikita Khrushchev

(c) John F. Kennedy

(d) Fidel Kennedy

5. The western alliance represented the ideology of -

(a) Socialism and communism

(b) Liberal democracy and capitalism

(c) Socialism and capitalism

(d) Liberal democracy and communism

6. Which one of the four doesn't form a group?

(a) US

(b) Britain

(c) France

(d) Germany

7. Second World War has spread in which of the following regions?

(a) Southeast Asia

(b) China

(c) Burma

(d) All of the above

8. The time period of the First World War is-

(a) 1914 and 1917

(b) 1913 and 1918

(c) 1914 and 1918

(d) 1913 and 1917

9. Hiroshima and Nagasaki cities belong to which of the following country?

(a) China

(b) Burma

(c) Japan

(d) India

10. The western alliance was formalised into an organisation, called__________.

(a) North Atlantic Treaty Organisation

(b) North American Treaty Organisation

(c) North Atlantic Trade Organisation

(d) South Atlantic Treaty Organisation

11. Warsaw pact member includes which of the following countries?

(a) Poland

(b) Hungary

(c) Romania

(d) All of the above

12. The Southeast Asian Treaty Organisation (SEATO) and the Central Treaty Organisation (CENTO) is formed by which of the following country?

(a) Soviet union

(b) United States

(c) China

(d) Europe

13. Which of the following leaders are the founding members of NAM?

(a) Jawaharlal Nehru

(b) Josip Broz Tito

(c) Sukarno

(d) All of the above

Level – 2

14. Which of the following factors are not the reasons behind formation of NAM?

(a) Cooperation among the five countries.

(b) Growing Cold War tensions and its widening arenas.

(c) The dramatic entry of many newly decolonised African countries into the inter-national arena. By 1960, there were 16 new African members in the UN.

(d) None of the above

15. The polity behind NAM is -
(a) Isolationism
(b) Neutrality
(c) Bipolarity
(d) None of the above

16. A report named Towards a New Trade Policy for Development is published by whom?
(a) NAM
(b) UNCTAD
(c) NATO
(d) WHO

17. Limited Test Ban Treaty was signed by which of the following countries?
(a) US
(b) UK
(c) USSR
(d) All of the above

18. Which of the following country is not a member of Nuclear Non-Proliferation Treaty?
(a) Britain
(b) France
(c) Belarus
(d) China

Answer Keys

Level – 1

1. (d)   2. (a)   3. (b)   4. (a)   5. (b)   6. (d)   7. (d)   8. (c)   9. (c)   10. (a)

11. (d)   12. (b)   13. (d)

Level – 2

14. (d)   15. (d)   16. (b)   17. (d)   18. (c)

Solutions

Level – 1

1. d The end of the Cold War is usually seen as the beginning of the contemporary era in world politics.

2. a The non-aligned countries establish a New International Economic Order (NIEO) as a means of attaining economic development and political independence.

3. b The Battle of Iwo Jima, Japan was fought on 23 February 1945.

4. a In April 1961, the leaders of the Union of Soviet Socialist Republics (USSR) were worried that the United States of America (USA) would invade communist-ruled Cuba and overthrow Fidel Castro, the president of the small island nation off the coast of the United States.

5. b The western alliance, headed by the US, represented the ideology of liberal democracy and capitalism while the eastern alliance, headed by the Soviet Union, was committed to the ideology of socialism and communism.

6. d In 1945, the Allied Forces, led by the US, Soviet Union, Britain and France defeated the Axis Powers led by Germany, Italy and Japan, ending the Second World War (1939-1945).

7. d The war had involved almost all the major powers of the world and spread out to regions outside Europe including Southeast Asia, China, Burma (now Myanmar) and parts of India's northeast.

8. c The First World War had earlier shaken the world between 1914 and 1918.

9. c The end of the Second World War was also the beginning of the Cold War. The world war ended when the United States dropped two atomic bombs on the Japanese cities of Hiroshima and Nagasaki in August 1945, causing Japan to surrender.

10. a The western alliance was formalised into an organisation, the North Atlantic Treaty Organisation (NATO), which came into existence in April 1949.

11. d

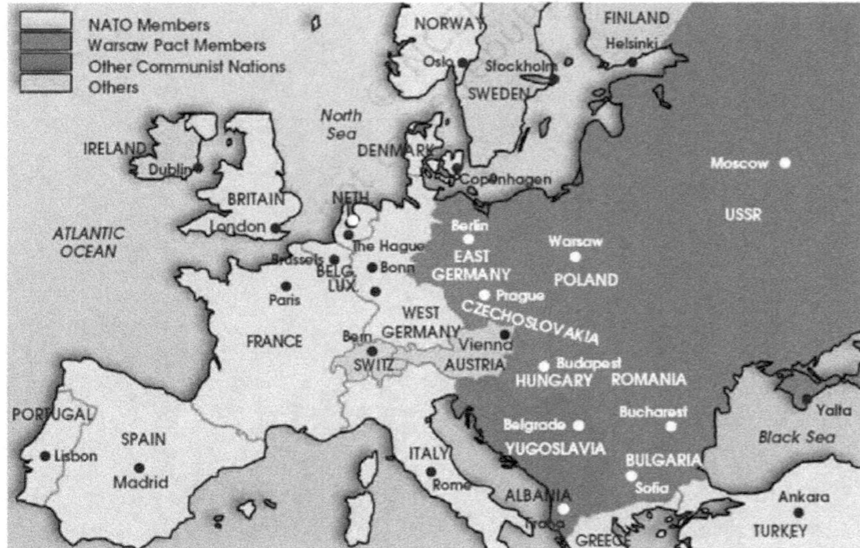

Map showing the way Europe was divided into rival alliances during the Cold War

12. b In East and Southeast Asia and in West Asia (Middle East), the United States built an alliance system called - the Southeast Asian Treaty Organisation (SEATO) and the Central Treaty Organisation (CENTO).

13. d Founding members of NAM are Josip Broz Tito, Jawaharlal Nehru, Gamal Abdel Nasser, Sukarno and Kwame Nkrumah.

Level – 2

14. d Nam was culmination of at least three factors:

   i.   cooperation among these five countries,

   ii. growing Cold War tensions and its widening arenas, and

   iii. the dramatic entry of many newly decolonised African countries into the inter - national arena. By 1960, there were 16 new African members in the UN.

15. d The policy of staying away from alliances should not be considered isolationism or neutrality. Non-alignment is not isolationism since isolationism means remaining aloof from world affairs. Isolationism sums up the foreign policy of the US from the American War of Independence in 1787 up to the beginning of the First World War. Neutrality refers principally to a policy of staying out of war. States practicing neutrality are not required to help end a war. They do not get involved in wars and do not take any position on the appropriateness or morality of a war.

16. b The United Nations Conference on Trade and Development (UNCTAD) brought out a report in 1972 entitled Towards a New Trade Policy for Development. The report proposed a reform of the global trading system so as to:

  (i) give the LDCs control over their natural resources exploited by the developed Western countries,

  (ii) obtain access to Western markets so that the LDCs could sell their products and, therefore, make trade more beneficial for the poorer countries,

  (iii) reduce the cost of technology from the Western countries, and

  (iv) provide the LDCs with a greater role in international economic institutions.

17. d Limited Test Ban Treaty (LTBT): Banned nuclear weapon tests in the atmosphere, in outer space and under water. Signed by the US, UK and USSR in Moscow on 5 August 1963. Entered into force on 10 October 1963.

18. c Nuclear Non-proliferation Treaty (NPT): Allows only the nuclear weapon states to have nuclear weapons and stops others from aquiring them. For the purposes of the NPT, a nuclear weapon state is one which has manufactured and exploded a nuclear weapon or other nuclear explosive device prior to 1 January 1967. So there are five nuclear weapon states: US, USSR (later Russia), Britain, France and China. Signed in Washington, London, and Moscow on 1 July 1968. Entered into force on 5 March 1970. Extended indefinitely in 1995.

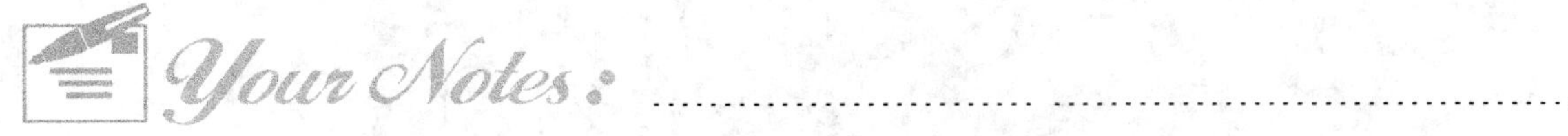
Your Notes: ....

CHAPTER 2

The End of Bipolarity

The Berlin Wall symbolised the division between the capitalist and the communist world. Built in 1961 to separate East Berlin from West Berlin, this more than 150 kilometre long wall stood for 28 years and was finally broken by the people on 9 November 1989. This marked the unification of the two parts of Germany and the beginning of the end of the communist bloc.

Vladimir Lenin (1870-1924) - Founder of the Bolshevik Communist party; leader of the Russian Revolution of 1917 and the founder-head of the USSR during the most difficult period following the revolution (1917-1924); an outstanding theoretician and practitioner of Marxism and a source of inspiration for communists all over the world.

Soviet System: The Union of Soviet Socialist Republics (USSR) came into being after the socialist revolution in Russia in 1917. The revolution was inspired by the ideals of socialism, as opposed to capitalism, and the need for an egalitarian society. After the Second World War, the east European countries that the Soviet army had liberated from the fascist forces came under the control of the USSR. The political and the economic systems of all these countries were modeled after the USSR. This group of countries was called the Second World or the 'socialist bloc'. The Warsaw Pact, a military alliance, held them together. The USSR was the leader of the bloc. The Soviet state ensured a minimum standard of living for all citizens, and the government subsidised basic necessities including health, education, childcare and other welfare schemes. There was no unemployment. State ownership was the dominant form of ownership: land and productive assets were owned and controlled by the Soviet state. The Soviet system, however, became very bureaucratic and authoritarian, making life very difficult for its citizens. The Soviet Union lagged behind the West in technology, infrastructure (e.g., transport, power), and most importantly, in fulfilling the political or economic aspirations of citizens. The Soviet invasion of Afghanistan in 1979 weakened the system even further. The Soviet economy was faltering in the late 1970s and became stagnant.

Joseph Stalin (1879-1953): Successor to Lenin and led the Soviet Union during its consolidation (1924-53); began rapid industrialization and forcible collectivisation of agriculture; credited with Soviet victory in the Second World War; held responsible for the Great Terror of the 1930s, authoritarian functioning and elimination of rivals within the party.

In December 1991, under the leadership of Yeltsin, Russia, Ukraine and Belarus, three major republics of the USSR, declared that the Soviet Union was disbanded. The Communist Party of the Soviet Union was banned. Capitalism and democracy were adopted as the bases for the post-Soviet republics. The declaration on the disintegration of the USSR and the formation of the Commonwealth of Independent States (CIS) came as a surprise to the other republics, especially to the Central Asian ones. The exclusion of these republics was an issue that was quickly solved by making them founding members of the CIS. Russia was now accepted as the successor state of the Soviet Union. It inherited the Soviet seat in the UN Security Council. Russia accepted all the international treaties and commitments of the Soviet Union. It took over as the only nuclear state of the post-Soviet space and carried out some nuclear disarmament measures with the US. The old Soviet Union was thus dead and buried.

The internal weaknesses of Soviet political and economic institutions, which failed to meet the aspirations of the people, were responsible for the collapse of the system. Economic stagnation for many years led to severe consumer shortages and a large section of Soviet society began to doubt and question the system and to do so openly.

The Soviet Union had become stagnant in an administrative and political sense as well. The Communist Party that had ruled the Soviet Union for over 70 years was not accountable to the people. Ordinary people were alienated by slow and stifling administration, rampant corruption, the inability of the system to correct mistakes it had made, the unwillingness to allow more openness in government, and the centralization of authority in a vast land. Worse still, the party bureaucrats gained more privileges than ordinary citizens. People did not identify with the system and with the rulers, and the government increasingly lost popular backing.

The rise of nationalism and the desire for sovereignty within various republics including Russia and the Baltic Republics (Estonia, Latvia and Lithuania), Ukraine, Georgia, and others proved to be the final and most immediate cause for the disintegration of the USSR.

1991 September: Three Baltic republics of Estonia, Latvia and Lithuania become UN members (later join NATO in March 2004).

1991 December: Russia, Belarus and Ukraine decide to annul the 1922 Treaty on the Creation of the USSR and establish the Commonwealth of Independent States (CIS); Armenia, Azerbaijan, Moldova, Kazakhstan, Kyrgyzstan, Tajikistan, Turkmenistan and Uzbekistan join the CIS (Georgia joins later in 1993); Russia takes over the USSR seat in the United Nations.

Shock Therapy in Post-communist Regimes: The collapse of communism was followed in most of these countries by a painful process of transition from an authoritarian socialist system to a democratic capitalist system. The model of transition in Russia, Central Asia and east Europe that was influenced by the World Bank and the IMF came to be known as 'shock therapy'. Each of these countries was required to make a total shift to a capitalist economy, which meant rooting out completely any structures evolved during the Soviet period. Above all, it meant that private ownership was to be the dominant pattern of ownership of property. Privatisation of state assets and corporate ownership patterns were to be immediately brought in. Collective farms were to be replaced by private farming and capitalism in agriculture. This transition ruled out any alternate or 'third way', other than state-controlled socialism or capitalism. Shock therapy also involved a drastic change in the external orientation of these economies. The free trade regime and foreign direct investment (FDI) were to be the main engines of change. This also involved openness to foreign investment, financial opening up or deregulation, and currency convertibility. Finally, the transition also involved a breakup of the existing trade alliances among the countries of the Soviet bloc. Each state from this bloc was now linked directly to the West and not to each other in the region. These states were thus to be gradually absorbed into the Western economic system.

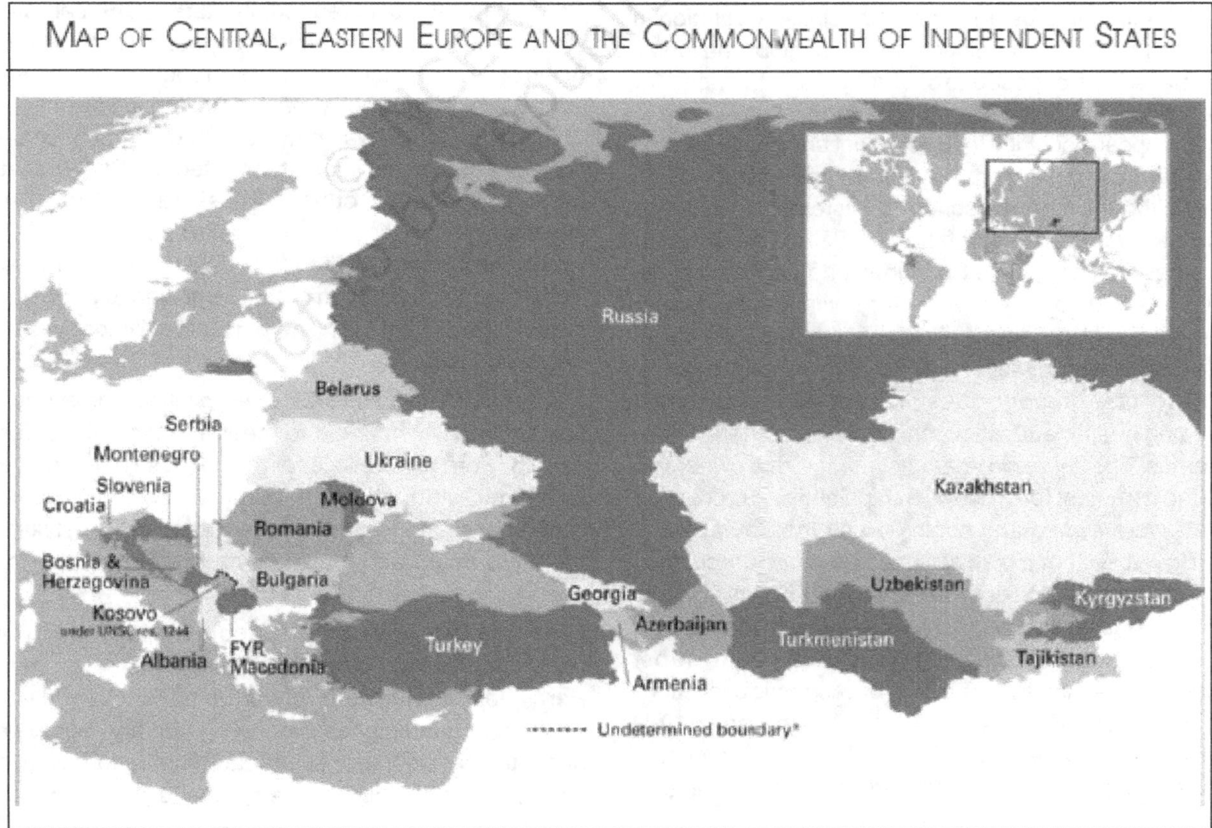

Consequences of Shock Therapy: Generally, it brought ruin to the economies and disaster upon the people of the entire region. In Russia, the large state-controlled industrial complex almost collapsed, as about 90 per cent of its industries were put up for sale to private individuals and companies. Since the restructuring was carried out through market forces and not by government-directed industrial policies, it led to the virtual disappearance of entire industries. This was called 'the largest garage sale in history', as valuable industries were undervalued and sold at throwaway prices. The value of the ruble, the Russian currency, declined dramatically. The rate of inflation was so high that people lost all their savings. The collective farm system disintegrated leaving people without food security, and Russia started to import food. The real GDP of Russia in 1999 was below what it was in 1989. The old trading structure broke down with no alternative in its place. The old system of social welfare was systematically destroyed. The withdrawal of government subsidies pushed large sections of the people into poverty. The middle classes were pushed to the periphery of society, and the academic and intellectual manpower disintegrated or migrated. A mafia emerged in most of these countries and started controlling many economic activities. The construction of democratic institutions was not given the same attention and priority as the demands of economic transformation. The constitutions of all these countries were drafted in a hurry and most, including Russia, had a strong executive president with the widest possible powers that rendered elected parliaments relatively weak. In Central Asia, the presidents had great powers, and several of them became very authoritarian.

Most of these economies, especially Russia, started reviving in 2000, ten years after their independence. The reason for the revival for most of their economies was the export of natural resources like oil, natural gas and minerals. Azerbaijan, Kazakhstan, Russia, Turkmenistan and Uzbekistan are major oil and gas producers. Other countries have gained because of the oil pipelines that cross their territories for which they get rent.

In Russia, two republics, Chechnya and Dagestan, have had violent secessionist movements. Moscow's method of dealing with the Chechen rebels and indiscriminate military bombings have led to many human rights violations but failed to deter the aspirations for independence.

In Central Asia, Tajikistan witnessed a civil war that went on for ten years till 2001. The region as a whole has many sectarian conflicts. In Azerbaijan's province of Nagorno-Karabakh, some local Armenians want to secede and join Armenia. In Georgia, the demand for independence has come from two provinces, resulting in a civil war. There are movements against the existing regimes in Ukraine, Kyrgyzstan and Georgia. Countries and provinces are fighting over river waters.

In Eastern Europe, Czechoslovakia split peacefully into two, with the Czechs and the Slovaks forming independent countries. But the most severe conflict took place in the Balkan republics of Yugoslavia. After 1991, it broke apart with several provinces like Croatia, Slovenia and Bosnia and Herzegovina declaring independence. Ethnic Serbs opposed this, and a massacre of non-Serb Bosnians followed. The NATO intervention and the bombing of Yugoslavia followed the inter-ethnic civil war.

India and Post-communist Countries: India has maintained good relations with all the post-communist countries. Russia and India share a vision of a multipolar world order. What they mean by a multipolar world order is the co-existence of several powers in the international system, collective security (in which an attack on any country is regarded as a threat to all countries and requires a collective response), greater regionalism, negotiated settlements of international conflicts, an independent foreign policy for all countries, and decision making through bodies like the UN that should be strengthened, democratised, and empowered. More than 80 bilateral agreements have been signed between India and Russia as part of the Indo-Russian Strategic Agreement of 2001. India is seeking to increase its energy imports from Russia and the republics of Kazakhstan and Turkmenistan.

The Soviet Union assisted India's public sector companies at a time when such assistance was difficult to get. It gave aid and technical assistance for steel plants like Bhilai, Bokaro, Visakhapatnam, and machinery plants like Bharat Heavy Electricals Ltd., etc. The Soviet Union accepted Indian currency for trade when India was short of foreign exchange.

The Soviet Union supported India's positions on the Kashmir issue in the UN. It also supported India during its major conflicts, especially during the war with Pakistan in 1971.

Exercise

Level – 1

1. Who was the leader of the Russian Revolution of 1917?

(a) Vladimir Lenin   (b) Joseph Stalin

(c) Nikita Khrushchev (d) Leonid Brezhnev

2. Which pact held together the east European countries and the USSR?

(a) Socialist Pact   (b) Warsaw Pact

(c) Tripartite Pact   (d) USSR Pact

3. Which were the three countries who disbanded Soviet Union?

(a) Russia, Ukraine and Turkmenistan

(b) Turkmenistan, Ukraine and Belarus

(c) Russia, Ukraine and Belarus

(d) Ukraine, Belarus and Latvia

4. Berlin Wall falls in which year?

(a) 1985   (b) 1986

(c) 1988   (d) 1989

5. Which was the first country of the 15 Soviet republics to declare its independence?

(a) Estonia   (b) Lithuania

(c) Latvia   (d) Belarus

6. Who was the first elected president of Russia?

(a) Boris Yeltsin

(b) Mikhail Gorbachev

(c) Leonid Brezhnev

(d) Vladimir Lenin

Level – 2

7. The collapse of the second world of the Soviet Union means -

(a) It meant the end of Cold War confrontations.

(b) Power relations in world politics changed and, therefore, the relative influence of ideas and institutions also changed.

(c) The end of the Soviet bloc meant the emergence of many new countries.

(d) All of the above.

8. The model of transition in Russia, Central Asia and east Europe was influenced by which of the following oraganisation?

(a) World Bank

(b) IMF

(c) Both (a) and (b)

(d) Neither (a) nor (b)

9. Which of the following are not the consequences of Shock Therapy?

(a) It brought prosperity to the economies and satisfaction to the people of the entire region.

(b) This was called 'the largest garage sale in history', as valuable industries were undervalued and sold at throwaway prices.

(c) The value of the ruble, the Russian currency, declined dramatically.

(d) The middle classes were pushed to the periphery of society, and the academic and intellectual manpower disintegrated or migrated.

10. Which of the following countries are major producers of oil and gas?

(a) Azerbaijan

(b) Uzbekistan

(c) Kazakhstan

(d) All of the above

11. Moscow's method of dealing with rebels is related to which of the following republic?

(a) Dagestan

(b) Chechnya

(c) Nagorno-Karabakh

(d) Georgia

12. Which of the following country supported India during the war with Pakistan in 1971?

(a) Georgia   (b) Armenia

(c) Russia   (d) Turkmenistan

Answer Keys

Level – 1

1. (a)   2. (b)   3. (c)   4. (d)   5. (b)   6. (a)

Level – 2

7. (d)   8. (c)   9. (a)   10. (d)   11. (b)   12. (c)

Solutions

Level – 1

1. a Vladimir Lenin (1870-1924) - Founder of the Bolshevik Communist party; leader of the Russian Revolution of 1917 and the founder-head of the USSR during the most difficult period following the revolution (1917-1924); an outstanding theoretician and practitioner of Marxism and a source of inspiration for communists all over the world.

2. b After the Second World War, the east European countries that the Soviet army had liberated from the fascist forces came under the control of the USSR. The political and the economic systems of all these countries were modeled after the USSR. This group of countries was called the Second World or the 'socialist bloc'. The Warsaw Pact, a military alliance, held them together. The USSR was the leader of the bloc.

3. c In December 1991, under the leadership of Yeltsin, Russia, Ukraine and Belarus, three major republics of the USSR, declared that the Soviet Union was disbanded. The Communist Party of the Soviet Union was banned.

4. d The Berlin Wall, which had been built at the height of the Cold War and was its greatest symbol, was toppled by the people in 1989.

5. b Lithuania becomes the first of the 15 Soviet republics to declare its independence in March, 1990.

6. a Boris Yeltsin (1931-2007): The first elected President of Russia (1991-1999); rose to power in the Communist Party and was made the Mayor of Moscow by Gorbachev; later joined the critics of Gorbachev and left the Communist Party; led the protests against the Soviet regime in 1991; played a key role in dissolving the Soviet Union; blamed for hardships suffered by Russians in their transition from communism to capitalism. the end of the Soviet bloc meant the emergence of many new countries.

Level – 2

7. d The collapse of the second world of the Soviet Union and the socialist systems in Eastern Europe had profound consequences for world politics. First of all, it meant the end of Cold War confrontations. Second, power relations in world politics changed and, therefore, the relative influence of ideas and institutions also changed. The end of the Cold War left open only two possibilities: either the remaining superpower would dominate and create a unipolar system, or different countries or groups of countries could become important players in the international system, thereby bringing in a multipolar system where no one power could dominate. Third, the end of the Soviet bloc meant the emergence of many new countries. All these countries had their own independent aspirations and choices.

8. c The collapse of communism was followed in most of these countries by a painful process of transition from an authoritarian socialist system to a democratic capitalist system. The model of transition in Russia, Central Asia and east Europe that was influenced by the World Bank and the IMF came to be known as 'shock therapy'.

9. a Generally, it brought ruin to the economies and disaster upon the people of the entire region. In Russia, the large state-controlled industrial complex almost collapsed, as about 90 per cent of its industries were put up for sale to private individuals and companies. Since the restructuring was carried out through market forces and not by government-directed industrial policies, it led to the virtual disappearance of entire industries. This was called 'the largest garage sale in history', as valuable industries were undervalued and sold at throwaway prices. The value of the ruble, the Russian currency, declined dramatically. The rate of inflation was so high that people lost all their savings. The collective farm system disintegrated leaving people without food security, and Russia started to import food. The real GDP of Russia in 1999 was below what it was in 1989. The old trading structure broke down with no alternative in its place. The old system of social welfare was systematically destroyed. The withdrawal of government subsidies pushed large sections of the people into poverty. The middle classes were pushed to the periphery of society, and the academic and intellectual manpower disintegrated or migrated. A mafia emerged in most of these countries and started controlling many economic activities.

10. d Most of these economies, especially Russia, started reviving in 2000, ten years after their independence. The reason for the revival for most of their economies was the export of natural resources like oil, natural gas and minerals. Azerbaijan, Kazakhstan, Russia, Turkmenistan and Uzbekistan are major oil and gas producers. Other countries have gained because of the oil pipelines that cross their territories for which they get rent.

11. b In Russia, two republics, Chechnya and Dagestan, have had violent secessionist movements. Moscow's method of dealing with the Chechen rebels and indiscriminate military bombings have led to many human rights violations but failed to deter the aspirations for independence.

12. c The Soviet Union supported India's positions on the Kashmir issue in the UN. It also supported India during its major conflicts, especially during the war with Pakistan in 1971.

CHAPTER 3

US Hegemony in World Politics

The US hegemony began in 1991 after Soviet power disappeared from the international scene.

Beginning of the 'New World Order: In August 1990, Iraq invaded Kuwait, rapidly occupying and subsequently annexing it. After a series of diplomatic attempts failed at convincing Iraq to quit its aggression, the United Nations mandated the liberation of Kuwait by force. For the UN, this was a dramatic decision after years of deadlock during the Cold War. The US President George H.W. Bush hailed the emergence of a 'new world order'. A massive coalition force of 660,000 troops from 34 countries fought against Iraq and defeated it in what came to be known as the First Gulf War. UN operation, which was called 'Operation Desert Storm', was overwhelmingly American. The First Gulf War revealed the vast technological gap that had opened up between the US military capability and that of other states. The highly publicised use of so called 'smart bombs' by the US led some observers to call this a 'computer war'. Widespread television coverage also made it a 'video game war', with viewers around the world watching the destruction of Iraqi forces live on TV in the comfort of their living rooms.

The Clinton Years: Despite winning the First Gulf War, George H.W. Bush lost the US presidential elections of 1992 to William Jefferson (Bill) Clinton of the Democratic Party. Bill Clinton won again in 1996 and thus remained the president of the US for eight years. In foreign policy, the Clinton government tended to focus on 'soft issues' like democracy promotion, climate change and world trade rather than on the 'hard politics' of military power and security. In 1999, in response to Yugoslavian actions against the predominantly Albanian population in the province of Kosovo. The air forces of the NATO countries, led by the US, bombarded targets around Yugoslavia for well over two months, forcing the downfall of the government of Slobodan Milosevic and the stationing of a NATO force in Kosovo. Another significant US military action during the Clinton years was in response to the bombing of the US embassies in Nairobi, Kenya and Dar-es-Salaam, Tanzania in 1998. These bombings were attributed to Al-Qaeda, a terrorist organisation strongly influenced by extremist Islamist ideas. Within a few days of this bombing, President Clinton ordered Operation Infinite Reach, a series of cruise missile strikes on Al-Qaeda terrorist targets in Sudan and Afghanistan.

9/11 and the 'Global War on Terror: On 11 September 2001, nineteen hijackers hailing from a number of Arab countries took control of four American commercial aircraft shortly after takeoff and flew them into important buildings in the US. One airliner each crashed into the North and South Towers of the World Trade Centre in New York. A third aircraft crashed into the Pentagon building in Arlington, Virginia, where the US Defence Department is headquartered. The fourth aircraft, presumably bound for the Capitol building of the US Congress, came down in a field in Pennsylvania. The attacks have come to be known as "9/11". The attacks killed nearly three thousand persons. In terms of their shocking effect on Americans, they have been compared to the British burning of Washington, DC in 1814 and the Japanese attack on Pearl Harbour in 1941. However, in terms of loss of life, 9/11 was the most severe attack on US soil since the founding of the country in 1776. As a part of its 'Global War on Terror', the US launched 'Operation Enduring Freedom' against all those suspected to be behind this attack, mainly Al-Qaeda and the Taliban regime in Afghanistan. The US forces made arrests all over the world, often without the knowledge of the government of the persons being arrested, transported these persons across countries and detained them in secret prisons. Some of them were brought to Guantanamo Bay, a US Naval base in Cuba, where the prisoners did not enjoy the protection of international law or the law of their own country or that of the US. Even the UN representatives were not allowed to meet these prisoners.

The Iraq Invasion: On 19 March 2003, the US launched its invasion of Iraq under the codename 'Operation Iraqi Freedom'. More than forty other countries joined in the US-led 'coalition of the willing' after the UN refused to give its mandate to the invasion. The ostensible purpose of the invasion was to prevent Iraq from developing weapons of mass destruction (WMD). Since no evidence of WMD has been unearthed in Iraq, it is speculated that the invasion was motivated by other objectives, such as controlling Iraqi oilfields and installing a regime friendly to the US.

The first meaning of hegemony relates to the relations, patterns and balances of military capability between states.

An open world economy requires a hegemon or dominant power to support its creation and existence. The hegemon must possess both the ability and the desire to establish certain norms for order and must sustain the global structure.

The US share of the world economy remains an enormous 21 per cent. The US also accounts for almost 14 per cent of world trade, if intra-European Union trade is included in world trade data.

The Bretton Woods system, set up by the US after the Second World War, still constitutes the basic structure of the world economy.

The World Bank, International Monetary Fund (IMF) and World Trade Organisation (WTO) as the products of American hegemony.

This third sense of hegemony is about the capacity to 'manufacture consent'. Here, hegemony implies class ascendancy in the social, political and particularly ideological spheres. Hegemony arises when the dominant class or country can win the consent of dominated classes, by persuading the dominated classes to view the world in a manner favourable to the ascendancy of the dominant class.

Constraints on American Power: The first constraint is the institutional architecture of the American state itself. A system of division of powers between the three branches of government places significant brakes upon the unrestrained and immoderate exercise of America's military power by the executive branch. The second constraint on American power is also domestic in nature, and stems from the open nature of American society. The North Atlantic Treaty Organisation (NATO) is the biggest constrain of US.

India's Relationship with the US: After the collapse of the Soviet Union, India suddenly found itself friendless in an increasingly hostile international environment. However, these were also the years when India decided to liberalise its economy and integrate it with the global economy. This policy and India's impressive economic growth rates in recent years have made the country an attractive economic partner for a number of countries including the US. The US absorbs about 65 per cent of India's total exports in the software sector. 35 per cent of the technical staff of Boeing is estimated to be of Indian origin. 300,000 Indians work in Silicon Valley. 15 percent of all high-tech start-ups are by Indian-Americans.

No single power is anywhere near balancing the US militarily. A military coalition against the US is even less likely given the differences that exist among big countries like China, India, and Russia that have the potential to challenge US hegemony.

Instead of engaging in activities opposed to the hegemonic power, it may be advisable to extract benefits by operating within the hegemonic system. This is called the 'bandwagon' strategy.

Exercise

Level – 1

1. In which of the following year US Hegemony begin?

  (a) 1991   (b) 1992

  (c) 1993   (d) 1994

2. In which of the following year Iraq invaded Kuwait?

  (a) 1989   (b) 1990

  (c) 1991   (d) 1992

3. First Gulf War fought between which of the following countries?

  (a) Kuwait and US

  (b) Russia and US

  (c) UK and US

  (d) Iraq and US

4. UN operation on Iraq popularly known as -

  (a) Operation Kuwait

  (b) Operation Storm

  (c) Operation Desert Storm

  (d) Operation Iraq

5. First Gulf War is also known as -

  (a) Computer war

  (b) Video game war

  (c) Both (a) and (b)

  (d) Neither (a) nor (b)

6. Bill Clinton became president of US in which of the following year?

  (a) 1992

  (b) 1993

  (c) 1995

  (d) 1997

7. President Clinton ordered a series of cruise missile strikes on Al-Qaeda terrorist targets in Sudan and Afghanistan named -

  (a) Operation Finite Reach

  (b) Operation Infinite Reach

  (c) Operation Reach

  (d) Operation Infinite

8. In which year US established as a nation?

  (a) 1774   (b) 1775

  (c) 1776   (d) 1777

Level – 2

9. North and South Towers of the World Trade Centre in New York was bombarded on -

  (a) 11 September 2001

  (b) 11 September 2011

  (c) 12 September 2001

  (d) 13 September 2001

10. As a part of its 'Global War on Terror', the US launched which of the following operation?

  (a) Operation Freedom

  (b) Operation Enduring Freedom

  (c) Operation Global War on Terror

  (d) Operation Against Terror

11. Guantanamo Bay, a US Naval base is located in which of the following country?

  (a) US   (b) Afghanistan

  (c) Kenya   (d) Cuba

12. In which of the following year the US launched its invasion of Iraq under the codename 'Operation Iraqi Freedom'?

  (a) 2000   (b) 2001

  (c) 2003   (d) 2004

13. SLOCs stand for -

  (a) Sea-lanes of communication

  (b) Ship-lanes of communication

  (c) Social-lanes of communication

  (d) Sea-lines of communication

14. What does Hegemony mean in actual sense?

  (a) The meaning of hegemony relates to the relations, patterns and balances of military capability between states.

  (b) The meaning of hegemony relates to the economy.

  (c) Hegemony is about the capacity to 'manufacture consent'.

  (d) All of the above

15. Instead of engaging in activities opposed to the hegemonic power, it may be advisable to extract benefits by operating within the hegemonic system. This is called the _______ strategy.

  (a) Anti-hegemonic   (b) Bandwagon

  (c) Bretton Woods   (d) Hegemonic

Answer Keys

Level – 1

1. (a)   2. (b)   3. (d)   4. (c)   5. (c)   6. (a)   7. (b)   8. (c)

Level – 2

9. (a)   10. (b)   11. (d)   12. (c)   13. (a)   14. (d)   15. (b)

Solutions

Level – 1

1. a The US hegemony began in 1991 after Soviet power disappeared from the international scene.

2. b In August 1990, Iraq invaded Kuwait, rapidly occupying and subsequently annexing it.

3. d The US President George H.W. Bush hailed the emergence of a 'new world order'. A massive coalition force of 660,000 troops from 34 countries fought against Iraq and defeated it in what came to be known as the First Gulf War.

4. c UN operation on Iraq was called 'Operation Desert Storm'.

5. c The First Gulf War revealed the vast technological gap that had opened up between the US military capability and that of other states. The highly publicised use of so called 'smart bombs' by the US led some observers to call this a 'computer war'. Widespread television coverage also made it a 'video game war', with viewers around the world watching the destruction of Iraqi forces live on TV in the comfort of their living rooms.

6. a Despite winning the First Gulf War, George H.W. Bush lost the US presidential elections of 1992 to William Jefferson (Bill) Clinton of the Democratic Party. Bill Clinton won again in 1996 and thus remained the president of the US for eight years.

7. b President Clinton ordered Operation Infinite Reach, a series of cruise missile strikes on Al-Qaeda terrorist targets in Sudan and Afghanistan.

8. c US were founded as country in the year 1776.

Level – 2

9. a On 11 September 2001, nineteen hijackers hailing from a number of Arab countries took control of four American commercial aircraft shortly after takeoff and flew them into important buildings in the US. One airliner each crashed into the North and South Towers of the World Trade Centre in New York. A third aircraft crashed into the Pentagon building in Arlington, Virginia, where the US Defence Department is headquartered. The fourth aircraft, presumably bound for the Capitol building of the US Congress, came down in a field in Pennsylvania. The attacks have come to be known as "9/11".

10. b As a part of its 'Global War on Terror', the US launched 'Operation Enduring Freedom' against all those suspected to be behind this attack, mainly Al-Qaeda and the Taliban regime in Afghanistan.

11. d The US forces made arrests all over the world, often without the knowledge of the government of the persons being arrested, transported these persons across countries and detained them in secret prisons. Some of them were brought to Guantanamo Bay, a US Naval base in Cuba, where the prisoners did not enjoy the protection of international law or the law of their own country or that of the US. Even the UN representatives were not allowed to meet these prisoners.

12. c On 19 March 2003, the US launched its invasion of Iraq under the codename 'Operation Iraqi Freedom'. More than forty other countries joined in the US-led 'coalition of the willing' after the UN refused to give its mandate to the invasion. The ostensible purpose of the invasion was to prevent Iraq from developing weapons of mass destruction (WMD).

13. a The best examples of a global public good are sea-lanes of communication (SLOCs), the sea routes commonly used by merchant ships. Free trade in an open world economy would not be possible without open SLOCs.

14. d The first meaning of hegemony relates to the relations, patterns and balances of military capability between states. An open world economy requires a hegemon or dominant power to support its creation and existence. The hegemon must possess both the ability and the desire to establish certain norms for order and must sustain the global structure. This third sense of hegemony is about the capacity to 'manufacture consent'.

15. b Instead of engaging in activities opposed to the hegemonic power, it may be advisable to extract benefits by operating within the hegemonic system. This is called the 'bandwagon' strategy.

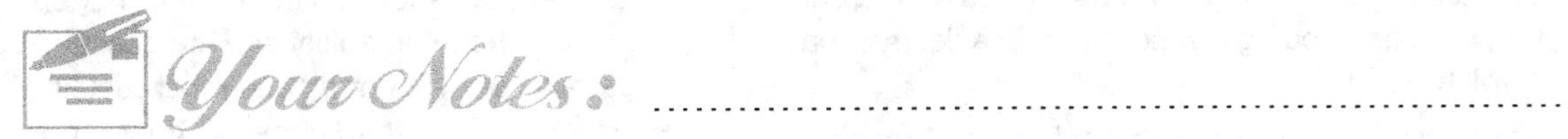
Your Notes :

CHAPTER 4

Alternative Centres of Power

European Union: In 1945, the European states confronted the ruin of their economies and the destruction of the assumptions and structures on which Europe had been founded. European integration after 1945 was aided by the Cold War. America extended massive financial help for reviving Europe's economy under what was called the 'Marshall Plan'. The US also created a new collective security structure under NATO. Under the Marshall Plan, the Organisation for European Economic Cooperation (OEEC) was established in 1948 to channel aid to the west European states. It became a forum where the western European states began to cooperate on trade and economic issues. The Council of Europe, established in 1949, was another step forward in political cooperation. The process of economic integration of European capitalist countries proceeded step by step leading to the formation of the European Economic Community in 1957. This process acquired a political dimension with the creation of the European Parliament. The collapse of the Soviet bloc put Europe on a fast track and resulted in the establishment of the European Union in 1992. The foundation was thus laid for a common foreign and security policy, cooperation on justice and home affairs, and the creation of a single currency. The EU has economic, political and diplomatic, and military influence. The EU is the world's second biggest economy with a GDP of more than \$17 trillion in 2016, next to that of the United States of America. Its currency, the euro, can pose a threat to the dominance of the US dollar. Its share of world trade is much larger than that of the United States allowing it to be more assertive in trade disputes with the US and China. Its economic power gives it influence over its closest neighbours as well as in Asia and Africa. It also functions as an important bloc in international of the EU, France, holds permanent seat on the UN Security Council. The EU includes several non-permanent members of the UNSC. Militarily, the EU's combined armed forces are the second largest in the world. Its total spending on defence is second after the US. Two EU member states, Britain and France, also have nuclear arsenals of approximately 550 nuclear warheads. It is also the world's second most important source of space and communications technology. As a supranational organisation, the EU is able to intervene in economic, political and social areas. But in many areas its member states have their own foreign relations and defence policies that are often at odds with each other. Thus, Britain's Prime Minister Tony Blair was America's partner in the Iraq invasion, and many of the EU's newer members made up the US led 'coalition of the willing' whereas Germany and France opposed American policy. There is also a deep-seated 'Euroskepticism' in some parts of Europe about the EU's integrationist agenda. Thus, for example, Britain's former Prime Minister, Margaret Thatcher, kept the UK out of the European Market. Denmark and Sweden have resisted the Maastricht Treaty and the adoption of the euro, the common European currency. This limits the ability of the EU to act in matters of foreign relations and defence.

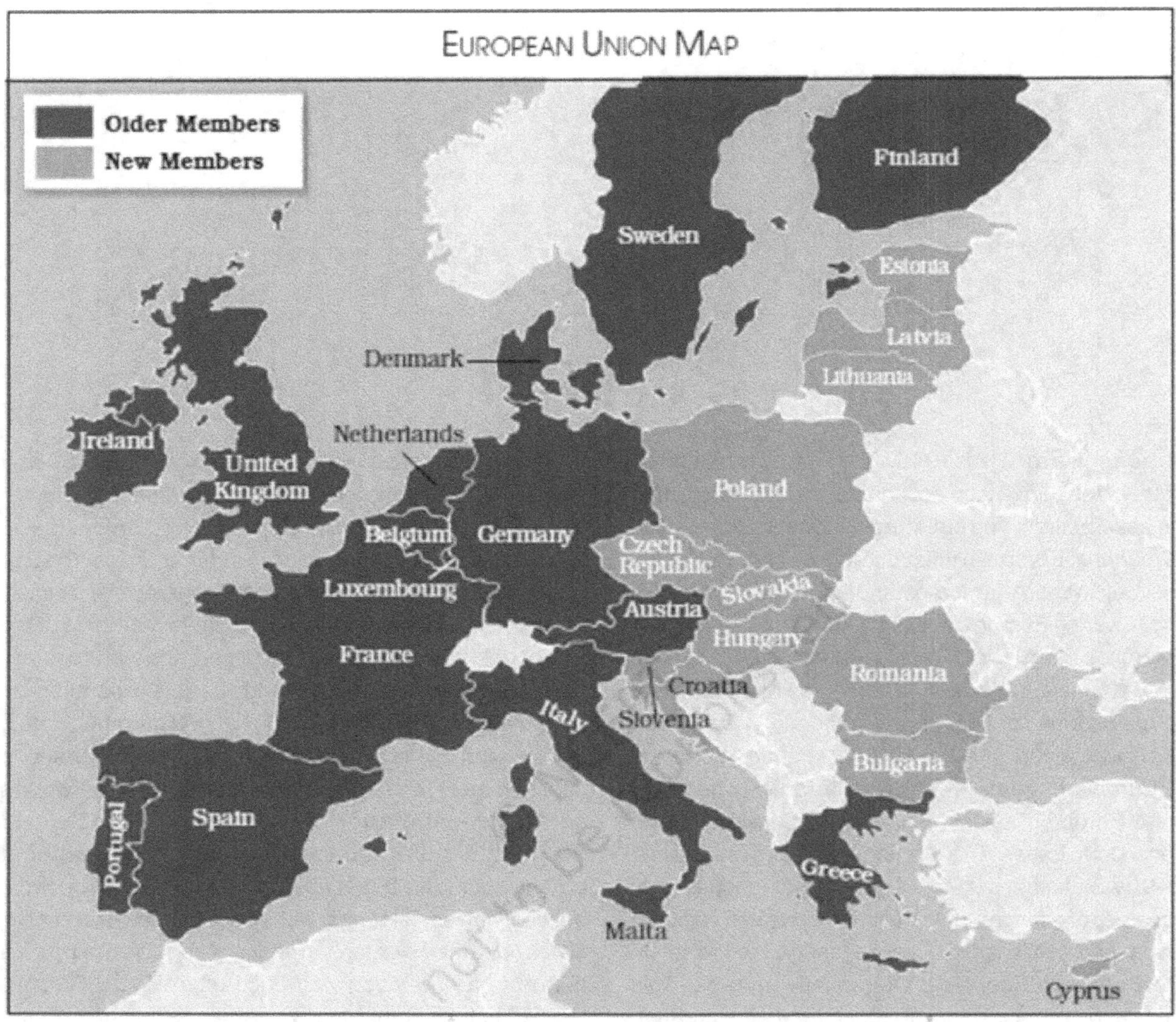

Association of South East Asian Nations (ASEAN): ASEAN was established in 1967 by five countries of this region - Indonesia, Malaysia, the Philippines, Singapore and Thailand - by signing the Bangkok Declaration. The objectives of ASEAN were primarily to accelerate economic growth and through that 'social progress and cultural development'. A secondary objective was to promote regional peace and stability based on the rule of law and the principles of the United Nations Charter. Over the years, Brunei Darussalam, Vietnam, Lao PDR, Myanmar (Burma) and Cambodia joined ASEAN taking its strength to ten. ASEAN countries have celebrated what has become known as the 'ASEAN Way', a form of interaction that is informal, non-confrontationist and cooperative. The respect for national sovereignty is critical to the functioning of ASEAN. With some of the fastest growing economies in the world, ASEAN broadened its objectives beyond the economic and social spheres. In 2003, ASEAN moved along the path of the EU by agreeing to establish an ASEAN Community comprising three pillars, namely, the ASEAN Security Community, the ASEAN Economic Community and the ASEAN Socio-Cultural Community. The ASEAN security community was based on the conviction that outstanding territorial disputes should not escalate into armed confrontation. By 2003, ASEAN had several agreements in place by which member states promised to uphold peace, neutrality, cooperation, non-interference, and respect for national differences and sovereign rights. The ASEAN Regional Forum (ARF), which was established in 1994, is the organisation that carries out coordination of security and foreign policy. ASEAN was and still remains principally an economic association. The objectives of the ASEAN Economic Community are to create a common market and production base within ASEAN states and to aid social and economic development in the region. The Economic Community would also like to improve the existing ASEAN Dispute Settlement Mechanism to resolve economic disputes. ASEAN has focused on creating a Free Trade Area (FTA) for investment, labour, and services. The US and China have already moved fast to negotiate FTAs with ASEAN. Its Vision 2020 has defined an outward-looking role for ASEAN in the international community. This builds on the existing ASEAN policy to encourage negotiation over conflicts in the region. Thus, ASEAN has mediated the end of the Cambodian conflict, the East Timor crisis, and meets annually to discuss East Asian cooperation. India signed trade agreements with three ASEAN members, Malaysia, Singapore and Thailand. The ASEAN-India FTA came into effect in 2010.

The Rise of the Chinese Economy: China's economic success since 1978 has been linked to its rise as a great power. China has been the fastest growing economy since the reforms first began there. It is projected to overtake the US as the world's largest economy by 2040. After the inception of the People's Republic of China in 1949, following the communist revolution under the leadership of Mao, its economy was based on the Soviet model. The economically backward communist China chose to sever its links with the capitalist world. It had little choice but to fall back on its own resources and, for a brief period, on Soviet aid and advice. The model was to create a state-owned heavy industries sector from the capital accumulated from agriculture. As it was short of foreign exchange that it needed in order to buy technology and goods on the world market, China decided to substitute imports by domestic goods. This model allowed China to use its resources to establish the foundations of an industrial economy on a scale that did not exist before. Employment and social welfare was assured to all citizens, and China moved ahead of most developing countries in educating its citizens and ensuring better health for them. The economy also grew at a respectable rate of 5-6 per cent. But an annual growth of 2-3 per cent in population meant that economic growth was insufficient to meet the needs of a growing population. Agricultural production was not sufficient to generate a surplus for industry. The Chinese leadership took major policy decisions in the 1970s. China ended its political and economic isolation

with the establishment of relations with the United States in 1972. Premier Zhou Enlai proposed the 'four modernisations' (agriculture, industry, science and technology and military) in 1973. By 1978, the then leader Deng Xiaoping announced the 'open door' policy and economic reforms in China. The policy was to generate higher productivity by investments of capital and technology from abroad. The privatisation of agriculture in 1982 was followed by the privatisation of industry in 1998. Trade barriers were eliminated only in Special Economic Zones (SEZs) where foreign investors could set up enterprises. In China, the state played and continues to play a central role in setting up a market economy. Privatisation of agriculture led to a remarkable rise in agricultural production and rural incomes. High personal savings in the rural economy lead to an exponential growth in rural industry. The Chinese economy, including both industry and agriculture, grew at a faster rate. The new trading laws and the creation of Special Economic Zones led to a phenomenal rise in foreign trade. China has become the most important destination for foreign direct investment (FDI) anywhere in the world. It has large foreign exchange reserves that now allow it to make big investment in other countries. China's accession to the WTO in 2001 has been a further step in its opening to the outside world. While the Chinese economy has improved dramatically, not everyone in China has received the benefits of the reforms. Unemployment has risen in China with nearly 100 million people looking for jobs. Female employment and conditions of work are as bad as in Europe of the eighteenth and nineteenth centuries. Environmental degradation and corruption have increased besides a rise in economic inequality between rural and urban residents and coastal and inland provinces.

India–China Relations: After India regained its independence from Britain, and China expelled the foreign powers, there was hope that both would come together to shape the future of the developing world and of Asia particularly. For a brief while, the slogan of 'Hindi-Chini bhaibhai' was popular. However, military conflict over a border dispute between the two countries marred that hope. Soon after independence, both states were involved in differences arising from the Chinese takeover of Tibet in 1950 and the final settlement of the Sino-Indian border. China and India were involved in a border conflict in 1962 over competing territorial claims principally in Arunachal

Pradesh and in the Aksai Chin region of Ladakh. A series of talks to resolve the border issue were also initiated in 1981. Rajiv Gandhi's visit to China in December 1988 provided the impetus for an improvement in India-China relations. Since then both governments have taken measures to contain conflict and maintain 'peace and tranquility' on the border. They have also signed agreements on cultural exchanges and cooperation in science and technology, and opened four border posts for trade. With India-China trade growing at 30 per cent per year since 1999, a more positive perspective on relations with China has emerged. Bilateral trade between India and China has increased from $338 million in 1992 to more than $84 billion in 2017. Recently the relation between the two countries has taken a downslide. Border disputes, China-Pakistan economic corridor and China's support to Pakistan in UN against India's move to counter terrorism are some of the factors for it.

Japan: Japan has very few natural resources and imports most of its raw materials. Even then it progressed rapidly after the end of the Second World War. Japan became a member of the Organisation for Economic Cooperation and Development (OECD) in 1964. In 2017, it is the third largest economy in the world. It is the only Asian member of the G-7. It is the eleventh most populous nation in the world. Japan is the only nation that suffered the destruction caused by nuclear bombs. It is the second largest contributor to the regular budget of the UN, contributing almost 10 per cent of the total. Japan has a security alliance with the US since 1951. As per Article 9 of the Japanese Constitution, "the Japanese people forever renounce war as a sovereign right of the nation and the threat or use of force as means of settling international disputes." Although Japan's military expenditure is only one per cent of its GDP, it is the seventh largest in the world.

South Korea: The Korean peninsula was divided into South Korea (Republic of Korea) and North Korea (Democratic People's Republic of Korea) at the end of the Second World War along the 38th Parallel. The Korean War during 1950-53 and dynamics of the Cold War era further intensified the rivalries between the two sides. Both the Koreas finally became Members of the UN on 17 September 1991. Meanwhile, South Korea emerged as a centre of power in Asia. Between the 1960s and the 1980s, it rapidly developed into an economic power, which is termed as "Miracle on the Han River". Signalling its all-round development, South Korea became a Member of the OECD in 1996. In 2017, its economy is the eleventh largest in the world and its military expenditure is the tenth largest. According to the Human Development Report 2016, the HDI rank of South Korea is 18. The major factors responsible for its high human development include "successful land reforms, rural development, extensive human resources development and rapid equitable economic growth." Other factors are export orientation, strong redistribution policies, public infrastructure development, effective institutions and governance. The South Korean brands such as Samsung, LG and Hyundai have become renowned in India. Numerous agreements between India and South Korea signify their growing commercial and cultural ties.

Exercise

1. ______________ is the organisation of ASEAN that deals with security.
   (a) ASEAN Security Community
   (b) ASEAN Economic Community
   (c) ASEAN Socio-Cultural Community
   (d) ASEAN Regional Forum

2. The Treaty of Maastricht was signed establishing the _________.
   (a) ASEAN   (b) ARF
   (c) EU   (d) WTO

3. Which of the following nations adopted an 'open door' policy?
   (a) China   (b) South Korea
   (c) Japan   (d) USA

4. The 'ASEAN Way' -
   (a) Reflects the life style of ASEAN members
   (b) A form of interaction among ASEAN members that is informal and cooperative
   (c) The defence policy followed by the ASEAN members
   (d) The road that connects all the ASEAN members

5. **Assertion:** The Korean peninsula was divided into South Korea (Republic of Korea) and North Korea (Democratic People's Republic of Korea) at the end of the Second World War along the 38th Parallel.

   Reason: The Korean War during 1950-53 and dynamics of the Cold War era further intensified the rivalries between the two sides.
   (a) Both the Assertion and the Reason are correct and the Reason is the correct explanation of the Assertion.
   (b) Both the Assertion and the Reason are correct but the Reason is not the correct explanation of the Assertion.
   (c) The Assertion is incorrect but the Reason is correct.
   (d) The Assertion is correct but the Reason is incorrect.

6. Consider the following statements about Japan:
   i. It is the second largest contributor to the regular budget of the UN, contributing almost 10 per cent of the total.
   ii. Japan became a member of the Organisation for Economic Cooperation and Development (OECD) in 1964.
   iii. In 2017, it is the third largest economy in the world.
   iv. It is the only Asian member of the G-7.

   Which of the statements given above are correct?
   (a) i and iii only   (b) ii and iv only
   (c) i, ii and iii only   (d) i, ii, iii and iv

7. 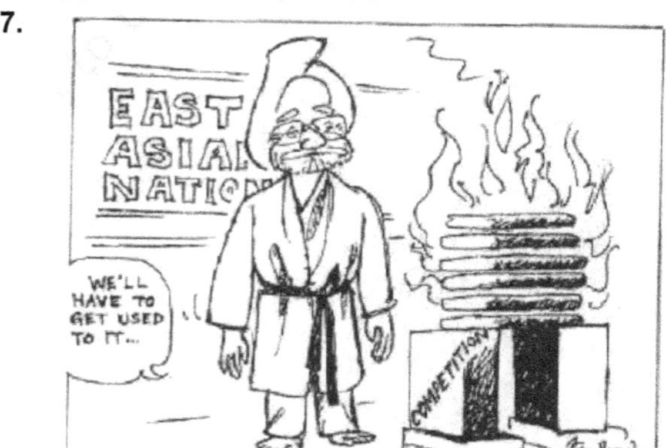

   Above given image depicts –
   (a) India's 'Look East' Policy since the early 1990s and 'Act East' Policy since 2014 that led to greater economic interaction with the East Asian nations.
   (b) Establishment of the ASEAN Regional Forum (ARF) in the year 1994.
   (c) Establishment of the Organisation for European Economic Cooperation (OEEC) in 1948.
   (d) China's accession to the WTO in 2001.

8. ______________ Plan influenced the establishment of the Organisation for European Economic Cooperation in 1948.
   (a) Marshall   (b) Regional
   (c) Economic   (d) Union

9. The border conflict between China and India in 1962 was principally over _______________ and _______________ region.
   (a) Arunachal Pradesh
   (b) Aksai Chin
   (c) Both
   (d) Neither

10. Arrange the following in chronological order:

   i.   China's accession to WTO

   ii. Establishment of the EEC

   iii. Establishment of the EU

   iv. Birth of ARF

   Select the correct answer using the code given below:

   (a) i-ii-iii-iv   (b) ii-iii-iv-i

   (c) iv-iii-ii-i   (d) i-iii-ii-iv

Answer Keys

1. (d)   2. (c)   3. (a)   4. (b)   5. (b)   6. (d)   7. (a)   8. (a)   9. (c)   10. (b)

CHAPTER 5

Contemporary South Asia

The expression 'South Asia' usually includes the following countries: Bangladesh, Bhutan, India, the Maldives, Nepal, Pakistan and Sri Lanka. The mighty Himalayas in the north and the vast Indian Ocean, the Arabian Sea and the Bay of Bengal in the south, west and east respectively provide a natural insularity to the region, which is largely responsible for the linguistic, social and cultural distinctiveness of the subcontinent. The boundaries of the region are not as clear in the east and the west, as they are in the north and the south. Afghanistan and Myanmar are often included in discussions of the region as a whole. China is an important player but is not considered to be a part of the region.

The various countries in South Asia do not have the same kind of political systems. Despite many problems and limitations, Sri Lanka and India have successfully operated a democratic system since their independence from the British. Pakistan and Bangladesh have experienced both civilian and military rulers, with Bangladesh remaining a democracy in the post-Cold War period. Pakistan began the post- Cold War period with successive democratic governments under Benazir Bhutto and Nawaz Sharif respectively. But it suffered a military coup in 1999. It has been run by a civilian government again since 2008. Till 2006, Nepal was a constitutional monarchy with the danger of the king taking over executive powers. In 2008, the monarchy was abolished and Nepal emerged as a democratic republic. Bhutan became a constitutional monarchy in 2008. Under the leadership of the king, it emerged as a multi-party democracy. The Maldives, the other island nation, was a Sultanate till 1968 when it was transformed into a republic with a presidential form of government. In June 2005, the parliament of the Maldives voted unanimously to introduce a multiparty system. The Maldivian Democratic Party (MDP) dominates the political affairs of the island. The MDP won the 2018 Elections.

The Military Democracy in Pakistan: After Pakistan framed its first constitution; General Ayub Khan took over the administration of the country and soon got himself elected. He had to give up office when there was popular dissatisfaction against his rule. This gave way to a military takeover once again under General Yahya Khan. During Yahya's military rule, Pakistan faced the Bangladesh crisis, and after a war with India in 1971, East Pakistan broke away to emerge as an independent country called Bangladesh. After this, an elected government under the leadership of Zulfikar Al Bhutto came to power in Pakistan from 1971 to 1977. The Bhutto government was removed by General Zia-ul-Haq in 1977. General Zia faced a pro-democracy movement from 1982 onwards and and an elected democratic government was established once again in 1988 under the leadership of Benazir Bhutto. This phase of elective democracy lasted till 1999 when the army stepped in again and General Pervez Musharraf removed Prime Minister Nawaz Sharif. In 2001, General Musharraf got himself elected as the President. Since 2008, democratically elected leaders have been ruling Pakistan. The social dominance of the military, clergy, and landowning aristocracy has led to the frequent overthrow of elected governments and the establishment of military government. Pakistan's conflict with India has made the pro-military groups more powerful.

Democracy in Bangladesh: Bangladesh was a part of Pakistan from 1947 to 1971. It consisted of the partitioned areas of Bengal and Assam from British India. The people of this region resented the domination of western Pakistan and the imposition of the Urdu language. Sheikh Mujibur Rahman led the popular struggle against West Pakistani domination. He demanded autonomy for the eastern region. In the 1970 elections in the then Pakistan, the Awami League led by Sheikh Mujib won all the seats in East Pakistan and secured a majority in the proposed constituent assembly for the whole of Pakistan. But the government dominated by the West Pakistani leadership refused to convene the assembly. Sheikh Mujib was arrested. Under the military rule of General Yahya Khan, the Pakistani army tried to suppress the mass movement of the Bengali people. Thousands were killed by the Pakistan army. This led to a large scale migration into India, creating a huge refugee problem for India. The government of India supported the demand of the people of East Pakistan for their independence and helped them financially and militarily. This resulted in a war between India and Pakistan in December 1971 that ended in the surrender of the Pakistani forces in East Pakistan and the formation of Bangladesh as an independent country. Bangladesh drafted its constitution declaring faith in secularism, democracy and socialism. However, in 1975 Sheikh Mujib got the constitution amended to shift from the parliamentary to presidential form of government. He also abolished all parties except his own, the Awami League. He was assassinated in a military uprising in August 1975. The new military ruler, Ziaur Rahman, formed his own Bangladesh National Party and won elections in 1979. He was assassinated and another military takeover followed under the leadership of Lt Gen H. M. Ershad. Since 1999 representative democracy based on multi-party elections has been working in Bangladesh.

Monarcy and Democracy in Nepal: Nepal was a Hindu kingdom in the past and then a constitutional monarchy in the modern period for many years. During the nineties, the Maoists of Nepal were successful in spreading their influence in many parts of Nepal. They believed in armed insurrection against the monarch and the ruling elite. This led to a violent conflict between the Maoist guerrillas and the armed forces of the king. For some time, there was a triangular conflict among the monarchist forces, the democrats and the Maoists. In 2002, the king abolished the parliament and dismissed the government, thus ending even the limited democracy that existed in Nepal. In 2008, Nepal became a democratic republic after abolishing the monarchy. In 2015, it adopted a new constitution.

Ethnic Conflict and Democracy in Sri Lanka: After its independence in 1948 politics in Sri Lanka (it was then known as Ceylon) was dominated by forces that represented the interest of the majority Sinhala community. They were hostile to a large number of Tamils who had migrated from India to Sri Lanka and settled there. This migration continued even after independence. The Sinhala nationalists thought that Sri Lanka should not give 'concessions' to the Tamils because Sri Lanka belongs to the Sinhala people only. The neglect of Tamil concerns led to militant Tamil nationalism. From 1983

onwards, the militant organisation, the Liberation Tigers of Tamil Eelam (LTTE) has been fighting an armed struggle with the army of Sri Lanka and demanding 'Tamil Eelam' or a separate country for the Tamils of Sri Lanka. The LTTE controls the northeastern parts of Sri Lanka. In 1987, the government of India for the first time got directly involved in the Sri Lankan Tamil question. India signed an accord with Sri Lanka and sent troops to stabilise relations between the Sri Lankan government and the Tamils. Eventually, the Indian Army got into a fight with the LTTE. The presence of Indian troops was also not liked much by the Sri Lankans. They saw this as an attempt by India to interfere in the internal affairs of Sri Lanka. In 1989, the Indian Peace Keeping Force (IPKF) pulled out of Sri Lanka without attaining its objective. The Sri Lankan crisis continued to be violent. However, international actors, particularly the Scandinavian countries such as Norway and Iceland tried to bring the warring groups back to negotiations. Finally, the armed conflict came to an end, as the LTTE was vanquished in 2009. Sri Lanka was one of the first developing countries to successfully control the rate of growth of population, the first country in the region to liberalise the economy, and it has had the highest per capita gross domestic product (GDP) for many years right through the civil war. Despite the ravages of internal conflict, it has maintained a democratic political system.

India-Pakistan Conflicts: Soon after the partition, the two countries got embroiled in a conflict over the fate of Kashmir. The Pakistani government claimed that Kashmir belonged to it. Wars between India and Pakistan in 1947-48 and 1965 failed to settle the matter. The 1947-48 war resulted in the division of the province into Pakistan-occupied Kashmir and the Indian province of Jammu and Kashmir divided by the Line of Control. In 1971, India won a decisive war against Pakistan but the Kashmir issue remained unsettled. India's conflict with Pakistan is also over strategic issues like the control of the Siachen glacier and over acquisition of arms. The arms race between the two countries assumed a new character with both states acquiring nuclear weapons and missiles to deliver such arms against each other in the 1990s. In 1998, India conducted nuclear explosion in Pokaran. Pakistan responded within a few days by carrying out nuclear tests in the Chagai Hills. The Indian government has blamed the Pakistan government for using a strategy of low-key violence by helping the Kashmiri militants with arms, training, money and protection to carry out terrorist strikes against India. The Indian government also believes that Pakistan had aided the pro-Khalistani militants with arms and ammunitions during the period 1985-1995. Its spy agency, Inter Services Intelligence (ISI), is alleged to be involved in various anti-India campaigns in India's northeast, operating secretly through Bangladesh and Nepal. In 1960, with the help of the World Bank, India and Pakistan signed the Indus Waters Treaty over the use of the rivers of the Indus basin. The two countries are not in agreement over the demarcation line in Sir Creek in the Rann of Kutch.

India and its Other Neighbours: The governments of India and Bangladesh have had differences over several issues including the sharing of the Ganga and Brahmaputra river waters. The Indian government has been unhappy with Bangladesh's denial of illegal immigration to India, its support for anti-Indian Islamic fundamentalist groups, Bangladesh's refusal to allow Indian troops to move through its territory to northeastern India, and its decision not to export natural gas to India or allow Myanmar to do so through Bangladeshi territory. Bangladesh is a part of India's Look East (Act East since 2014) policy that wants to link up with Southeast Asia via Myanmar. Nepal and India has a treaty between the two countries allows the citizens of the two countries to travel to and work in the other country without visas and passports. The Indian government has often expressed displeasure at the warm relationship between Nepal and China and at the Nepal government's inaction against anti-Indian elements. Indian security agencies see the Maoist movement in Nepal as a growing security threat, given the rise of Naxalite groups in various Indian states from Bihar in the north to Andhra Pradesh in the south. Many leaders and citizens in Nepal think that the Indian government interferes in its internal affairs, has designs on its river waters and hydro-electricity, and prevents Nepal, a landlocked country, from getting easier access to the sea through Indian Territory. India enjoys a very special relationship with Bhutan too and does not have any major conflict with the Bhutanese government. The efforts made by the Bhutanese monarch to weed out the guerrillas and militants from northeastern India that operate in his country have been helpful to India. India is involved in big hydroelectric projects in Bhutan and remains the Himalayan kingdom's biggest source of development aid. India's ties with the Maldives remain warm and cordial. In November 1988, when some Tamil mercenaries from Sri Lanka attacked the Maldives, the Indian air force and navy reacted quickly to the Maldives' request to help stop the invasion. Nepal and Bhutan, as well as Bangladesh and Myanmar, have had disagreements in the past over the migration of ethnic Nepalese into Bhutan and the Rohingyas into Myanmar, respectively. Bangladesh and Nepal have had some differences over the future of the Himalayan river waters.

Peace and Cooperation: The South Asian Association for Regional Cooperation (SAARC) is a major regional initiative by the South Asian states to evolve cooperation through multilateral means. It began in 1985. Unfortunately, due to persisting political differences, SAARC has not had much success. SAARC members signed the South Asian Free Trade (SAFTA) agreement which promised the formation of a free trade zone for the whole of South Asia. A new chapter of peace and cooperation might evolve in South Asia if all the countries in the region allow free trade across the borders. This is the spirit behind the idea of SAFTA. The Agreement was signed in 2004 and came into effect on 1 January 2006. SAFTA aims at lowering trade tariffs. China and the United States remain key players in South Asian politics. Sino-Indian relations have improved significantly in the last ten years, but China's strategic partnership with Pakistan remains a major irritant.

Exercise

1. South East includes which of the following countries?

   1. Bangladesh
   2. Bhutan
   3. India
   4. Maldives
   5. Nepal
   6. Pakistan
   7. Sri Lanka

   Select the correct answer using the code given below:

   (a) 1, 2, 3, 4 and 5 only

   (b) 2, 3, 4, 6 and 7 only

   (c) 1, 3, 5 and 7 only

   (d) 1, 2, 3, 4, 5, 6 and 7

2. Consider the following statements:

   1. The mighty Himalayas in the north and the vast Indian Ocean, the Arabian Sea and the Bay of Bengal in the south, west and east respectively provide a natural insularity to the region.
   2. China is an important part of this region.

   Which of the statements given above is/are correct about South East?

   (a) 1 only   (b) 2 only

   (c) Both 1 and 2   (d) Neither 1 nor 2

3. Which of the following pair of countries have faced both civilian and military rules?

   (a) India and Sri Lanka

   (b) Pakistan and India

   (c) Pakistan and Bangladesh

   (d) Bangladesh and Nepal

4. Till 2006, this country was a constitutional monarchy with the danger of the king taking over executive powers. In 2008, the monarchy was abolished and the country emerged as a democratic republic. Identify the country.

   (a) Bangladesh   (b) Nepal

   (c) Bhutan   (d) Maldives

5. East Pakistan was divided from West Pakistan in which of the following year?

   (a) 1970   (b) 1971

   (c) 1972   (d) 1973

6. Assertion: In Nepal there was a triangular conflict among the monarchist forces, the democrats and the Maoists.

   Reason: In 2002, the king abolished the parliament and dismissed the government, thus ending even the limited democracy that existed in Nepal.

   (a) Both the Assertion and the Reason are correct and the Reason is the correct explanation of the Assertion.

   (b) Both the Assertion and the Reason are correct but the Reason is not the correct explanation of the Assertion.

   (c) The Assertion is incorrect but the Reason is correct.

   (d) The Assertion is correct but the Reason is incorrect.

7. After its independence, politics in ___________ (it was then known as Ceylon) was dominated by forces that represented the interest of the majority Sinhala community.

   (a) Nepal

   (b) Bhutan

   (c) Sri Lanka

   (d) Maldives

8. **Assertion:** In 1998, India conducted nuclear explosion in Pokaran.

   Reason: Pakistan responded within a few days by carrying out nuclear tests in the Chagai Hills.

   (a) Both the Assertion and the Reason are correct and the Reason is the correct explanation of the Assertion.

   (b) Both the Assertion and the Reason are correct but the Reason is not the correct explanation of the Assertion.

   (c) The Assertion is incorrect but the Reason is correct.

   (d) The Assertion is correct but the Reason is incorrect.

9. Consider the following statements:

1. Bangladesh is a part of India's Look East (Act East since 2014) policy that wants to link up with Southeast Asia via Myanmar.
2. Nepal and India enjoy a very special relationship that has very few parallels in the world. A treaty between the two countries allows the citizens of the two countries to travel to and work in the other country without visas and passports.

Which of the statements given above is/are incorrect?

(a) 1 only   (b) 2 only

(c) Both 1 and 2   (d) Neither 1 nor 2

10. Which of the following statements are correct about the South Asian Association for Regional Cooperation (SAARC)?

1. It is a major regional initiative by the South Asian states to evolve cooperation through multilateral means.
2. SAARC members signed the South Asian Free Trade (SAFTA) agreement which promised the formation of a free trade zone for the whole of South Asia.
3. It began in 1985.

Select the correct answer using the code given below:

(a) 1 and 2 only   (b) 1 and 3 only

(c) 2 and 3 only   (d) 1, 2 and 3

Answer Keys

1. (d)   2. (a)   3. (c)   4. (b)   5. (b)   6. (b)   7. (c)   8. (b)   9. (d)   10. (d)

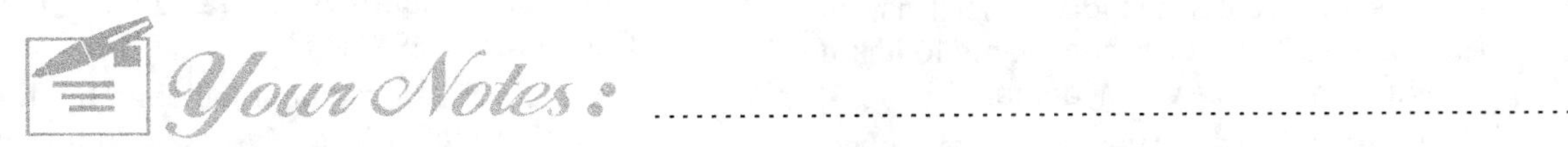

Your Notes :

International Organisations

An international organisation is not a super-state with authority over its members. It is created by and responds to states. It comes into being when states agree to its creation. Once created, it can help member states resolve their problems peacefully.

IMF: The International Monetary Fund (IMF) is an international organisation that oversees those financial institutions and regulations that act at the international level. The IMF has 189 member countries (as on 12 April 2016) but they do not enjoy an equal say. The G-7 members US (16.52%), Japan (6.15%), Germany (5.32%), France (4.03%), UK (4.03%), Italy (3.02%) and Canada (2.22%) have 41.29% of the votes. China (6.09%), India (2.64%), Russia (2.59%) Brazil (2.22%) and Saudi Arabia (2.02%) are the other major members.

Evolution of the UN: The First World War encouraged the world to invest in an international organisation to deal with conflict. Many believed that such an organisation would help the world to avoid war. As a result, the League of Nations was born. However, despite its initial success, it could not prevent the Second World War (1939-45). The UN was founded as a successor to the League of Nations. It was established in 1945 immediately after the Second World War. The organisation was set up through the signing of the United Nations Charter by 51 states. The UN's objective is to prevent international conflict and to facilitate cooperation among states. By 2011, the UN had 193 member states. These included almost all independent states. In the UN General Assembly, all members have one vote each. In the UN Security Council, there are five permanent members. These are: the United States, Russia, the United Kingdom, France and China. These states were selected as permanent members as they were the most powerful immediately after the Second World War and because they constituted the victors in the War. The present Secretary-General is António Guterres. He is the ninth Secretary-General of the UN. He took over as the Secretary-General on 1 January 2017. He was the Prime Minister of Portugal (1995-2002) and the UN High Commissioner for Refugees (2005-2015).

The UN consists of many different structures and agencies. War and peace and differences between member states are discussed in the General Assembly as well as the Security Council. Social and economic issues are dealt with by many agencies including the World Health Organisation (WHO), the United Nations Development Programme (UNDP), the United Nations Human Rights Commision (UNHRC), and the United Nations High Commission for Refugees (UNHCR), the United Nations Children's Fund (UNICEF), and the United Nations Educational, Scientific, and Cultural Organisation (UNESCO), among others.

Reform of the UN after the Cold War: Two basic kinds of reforms face the UN: reform of the organisation's structures and processes; and a review of the issues that fall within the jurisdiction of the organisation. On the reform of structures and processes the demand for an increase in the UN Security Council's permanent and non-permanent membership so that the realities of contemporary world politics are better reflected in the structure of the organisation. In particular, there are proposals to increase membership from Asia, Africa and South America. Beyond this, the US and other Western countries want improvements in the UN's budgetary procedures and its administration. On the issues to be given greater priority or to be brought within the jurisdiction of the UN, some countries and experts want the organisation to play a greater or more effective role in peace and security missions, while others want its role to be confined to development and humanitarian work (health, education, environment, population control, human rights, gender and social justice).

World Bank: The World Bank was created during the Second World War in 1944. Its activities are focused on the developing countries. It works for human development (education, health), agriculture and rural development (irrigation, rural services), environmental protection (pollution reduction, establishing and enforcing regulations), infrastructure (roads, urban regeneration, and electricity) and governance (anti-corruption, development of legal institutions). It provides loans and grants to the member-countries. In this way, it exercises enormous influence on the economic policies of developing countries. It is often criticised for setting the economic agenda of the poorer nations, attaching stringent conditions to its loans and forcing free market reforms.

Reform of Structures and Processes: A related issue was to change the nature of membership altogether. Some insisted, for instance, that the veto power of the five permanent members be abolished. Many perceived the veto to be in conflict with the concept of democracy and sovereign equality in the UN and thought that the veto was no longer right or relevant. In the Security Council, there are five permanent members and ten non-permanent members. The Charter gave the permanent members a privileged position to bring about stability in the world after the Second World War. The main privileges of the five permanent members are permanency and the veto power. The non-permanent members serve for only two years at a time and give way after that period to newly elected members. A country cannot be re-elected immediately after completing a term of two years. The non-permanent members are elected in a manner so that they represent all continents of the world. Most importantly, the non-permanent members do not have the veto power. What is the veto power? In taking decisions, the Security Council proceeds by voting. All members have one vote. However, the permanent members can vote in a negative manner so that even if all other permanent and non-permanent members vote for a particular decision, any permanent member's negative vote can stall the decision. This negative vote is the veto.

Establishment of a Human Rights Council (operational since 19 June 2006)

WTO: The World Trade Organisation (WTO) is an international organisation which sets the rules for global trade. This organisation was set up in 1995 as the successor to the General Agreement on Trade and Tariffs (GATT) created after the Second World War. It has 164 members (as on 29 July 2016). All decisions are taken unanimously but the major economic powers such as the US, EU and Japan has managed to use the WTO to frame rules of trade to advance their own interests. The developing countries often complain of non-transparent procedures and being pushed around by big powers.

IAEA: The International Atomic Energy Agency (IAEA) was established in 1957. It came into being to implement US President Dwight Eisenhower's "Atoms for Peace" proposal. It seeks to promote the peaceful use of nuclear energy and to prevent its use for military purposes. IAEA teams regularly inspect nuclear facilities all over the world to ensure that civilian reactors are not being used for military purposes.

Amnesty International: Amnesty International is an NGO that campaigns for the protection of human rights all over the world. It promotes respect for all the human rights in the Universal Declaration of Human Rights. It believes that human rights are interdependent and indivisible. It prepares and publishes reports on human rights. Governments are not always happy with these reports since a major focus of Amnesty is the misconduct of government authorities. Nevertheless, these reports play an important role in research and advocacy on human rights.

Human Rights Watch: Human Rights Watch is another international NGO involved in research and advocacy on human rights. It is the largest international human rights organisation in the US. It draws the global media's attention to human rights abuses. It helped in building international coalitions like the campaigns to ban landmines, to stop the use of child soldiers and to establish the International Criminal Court.

Exercise

1. World Bank was created in which of the following year?
   - (a) 1944
   - (b) 1943
   - (c) 1945
   - (d) 1946

2. Which of the following NGO related to human rights?
   - (a) Amnesty International
   - (b) Human Rights Watch
   - (c) Both (a) and (b)
   - (d) Neither (a) nor (b)

3. The prime objective of the UN is
   _______________________________.
   - (a) To maintain law and order
   - (b) To maintain harmony
   - (c) To maintain peace
   - (d) To maintain peace and security

4. The highest functionary of the UN is called_________________.
   - (a) President
   - (b) Executive
   - (c) Secretariat
   - (d) Chairman

5. The UN Security Council has ______ permanent and ______ non-permanent members.
   - (a) 10, 5
   - (b) 10, 20
   - (c) 5, 10
   - (d) 20, 10

6. WTO is serving as the successor to which of the following organization?
   - (a) General Agreement on Trade and Tariffs
   - (b) General Arrangement on Trade and Tariffs
   - (c) World Health Organisation
   - (d) UN Development Programme

7. The UN agency concerned with the safety and peaceful use of nuclear technology is:
   - (a) The UN Committee on Disarmament
   - (b) International Atomic Energy Agency
   - (c) UN International Safeguard Committee
   - (d) None of the above

8. Which among the following would give more weightage to India's proposal for permanent membership in the Security Council?
   - (a) Nuclear capability
   - (b) It has been a member of the UN since its inception
   - (c) It is located in Asia
   - (d) India's growing economic power and stable political system

9. Which of the following statements are correct about the way the UN functions?
   1. All security and peace related issues are dealt with in the Security Council.
   2. Humanitarian policies are implemented by the main organs and specialised agencies spread across the globe.
   3. Having consensus among the five permanent members on security issues is vital for its implementation.
   4. The members of the General Assembly are automatically the members of all other principal organs and specialised agencies of the UN.

   Select the correct answer using the code given below:
   - (a) 2 and 4 only
   - (b) 1 and 3 only
   - (c) 1 and 4 only
   - (d) 2 and 3 only

10. Consider the following statements about the veto power:
    1. Only the permanent members of the Security Council possess the veto power.
    2. It's a kind of negative power.
    3. The Secretary-General uses this power when not satisfied with any decision.
    4. One veto can stall a Security Council resolution.

    Which of the statements given above are correct?
    - (a) 1, 2 and 4 only
    - (b) 1, 2 and 3 only
    - (c) 2 and 4 only
    - (d) 1, 2, 3 and 4

Answer Keys

1. (a)	2. (c)	3. (d)	4. (c)	5. (c)	6. (a)	7. (b)	8. (d)	9. (b)	10. (a)

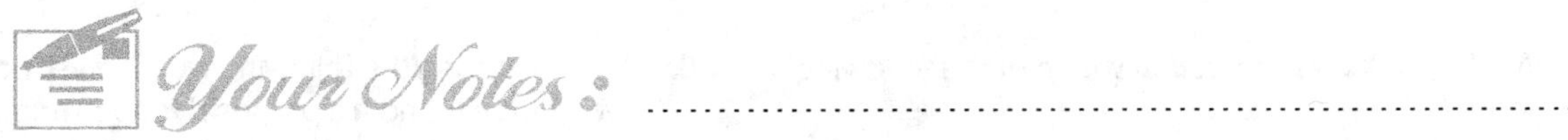

Your Notes :

Security in the Contemporary World

What is Security?: At its most basic, security implies freedom from threats. Security relates only to extremely dangerous threats-threats that could so endanger core values that those values would be damaged beyond repair if we did not do something to deal with the situation.

Traditional Notions: External: In the traditional conception of security, the greatest danger to a country is from military threats. The source of this danger is another country which by threatening military action endangers the core values of sovereignty, independence and territorial integrity. Military action also endangers the lives of ordinary citizens. Security policy is concerned with preventing war, which is called deterrence, and with limiting or ending war, which is called defence. Traditional security policy has a third component called balance of power. A good part of maintaining a balance of power is to build up one's military power, although economic and technological power are also important since they are the basis for military power. A fourth and related component of traditional security policy is alliance building. An alliance is a coalition of states that coordinate their actions to deter or defend against military attack. Most alliances are formalised in written treaties and are based on a fairly clear identification of who constitutes the threat. Countries form alliances to increase their effective power relative to another country or alliance. Alliances are based on national interests and can change when national interests change.

Traditional Notions: Internal: Traditional security must also, therefore, concern itself with internal security. As the colonies became free from the late 1940s onwards, their security concerns were often similar to that of the European powers. Some of the newly independent countries, like the European powers, became members of the Cold War alliances. They, therefore, had to worry about the Cold War becoming a hot war and dragging them into hostilities - against neighbours who might have joined the other side in the Cold War, against the leaders of the alliances (the United States or Soviet Union), or against any of the other partners of the US and Soviet Union. The Cold War between the two superpowers was responsible for approximately one-third of all wars in the post-Second World War period. Most of these wars were fought in the Third World. Just as the European colonial powers feared violence in the colonies, some colonial people feared, after independence, that they might be attacked by their former colonial rulers in Europe. They had to prepare, therefore, to defend themselves against an imperial war. The security challenges facing the newly-independent countries of Asia and Africa were different from the challenges in Europe in two ways. For one thing, the new countries faced the prospect of military conflict with neighbouring countries. For another, they had to worry about internal military conflict. These countries faced threats not only from outside their borders, mostly from neighbours, but also from within. Many newly independent countries came to fear their neighbours even more than they feared the US or Soviet Union or the former colonial powers. They quarrelled over borders and territories or control of people and populations or all of these simultaneously. Internal wars now make up more than 95 per cent of all armed conflicts fought anywhere in the world. Between 1946 and 1991, there was a twelve-fold rise in the number of civil wars-the greatest jump in 200 years. So, for the new states, external wars with neighbours and internal wars posed a serious challenge to their security.

Traditional Security and Cooperation: In traditional security, there is recognition that cooperation in limiting violence is possible. These limits relate both to the ends and the means of war. Traditional views of security do not rule out other forms of cooperation as well. The most important of these are disarmament, arms control, and confidence building. Disarmament requires all states to give up certain kinds of weapons. For example, the 1972

Biological Weapons Convention (BWC) and the 1992 Chemical Weapons Convention (CWC) banned the production and possession of these weapons. More than 155 states acceded to the BWC and 181 states acceded to the CWC. Both conventions included all the great powers. But the superpowers - the US and Soviet Union - did not want to give up the third type of weapons of mass destruction, namely, nuclear weapons, so they pursued arms control. Arms control regulates the acquisition or development of weapons. The Anti-ballistic Missile (ABM) Treaty in 1972 tried to stop the United States and Soviet Union from using ballistic missiles as a defensive shield to launch a nuclear attack. While it did allow both countries to deploy a very limited number of defensive systems, it stopped them from large-scale production of those systems. The US and Soviet Union signed a number of other arms control treaties including the Strategic Arms Limitations Treaty II or SALT II and the Strategic Arms Reduction Treaty (START). The Nuclear Non-Proliferation Treaty (NPT) of 1968 was an arms control treaty in the sense that it regulated the acquisition of nuclear weapons: those countries that had tested and manufactured nuclear weapons before 1967 were allowed to keep their weapons; and those that had not done so were to give up the right to acquire them. The NPT did not abolish nuclear weapons; rather, it limited the number of countries that could have them. Traditional security also accepts confidence building as a means of avoiding violence. Confidence building is a process in which countries share ideas and information with their rivals. Confidence building is a process designed to ensure that rivals do not go to war through misunderstanding or misperception.

Non-Traditional Notions: Non-traditional views of security have been called 'human security' or 'global security'. Human security is about the protection of people more than the protection of states. Human security and state security should be - and often are - the same thing. All proponents of human security agree that its primary goal is the protection of individuals. Proponents of the 'narrow' concept of human security focus on violent threats to individuals or, as former UN Secretary-General Kofi Annan puts it, "the protection of communities and individuals from internal violence". Proponents of the 'broad' concept of human security argue that the threat agenda should include hunger, disease and natural disasters because these kill far more people than war, genocide and terrorism combined. Human security policy, they argue, should protect people from these threats as well as from violence. In its broadest formulation, the human security agenda also encompasses economic security and 'threats to human dignity'. Put differently, the broadest formulation stresses what has been called

'freedom from want' and 'freedom from fear', respectively. The idea of global security emerged in the 1990s in response to the global nature of threats such as global warming, international terrorism, and health epidemics like AIDS and bird flu and so on.

New Sources of Threats: Terrorism refers to political violence that targets civilians deliberately and indiscriminately. International terrorism involves the citizens or territory of more than one country. Terrorist groups seek to change a political context or condition that they do not like by force or threat of force. Civilian targets are usually chosen to terrorise the public and to use the unhappiness of the public as a weapon against national governments or other parties in conflict. The classic cases of terrorism involve hijacking planes or planting bombs in trains, cafes, markets and other crowded places. Since 11 September 2001 when terrorists attacked the World Trade Centre in America, other governments and public have paid more attention to terrorism, though terrorism itself is not new. In the past, most of the terror attacks have occurred in the Middle East, Europe, Latin America and South Asia.

❖ **Human rights have come to be classified into three types.** The first type is political rights such as freedom of speech and assembly. The second type is economic and social rights. The third type is the rights of colonised people or ethnic and indigenous minorities. Since the 1990s, developments such as Iraq's invasion of Kuwait, the genocide in Rwanda, and the Indonesian military's killing of people in East Timor have led to a debate on whether or not the UN should intervene to stop human rights abuses.

❖ **Global poverty is another source of insecurity.** World population—now at 760 crore—will grow to nearly 1000 crore by the middle of the 21st century. Currently, half the world's population growth occurs in just six countries—India, China, Pakistan, Nigeria, Bangladesh and Indonesia. Among the world's poorest countries, population is expected to triple in the next 50 years, whereas many rich countries will see population shrinkage in that period. High per capita income and low population growth make rich states or rich social groups get richer, whereas low incomes and high population growth reinforce each other to make poor states and poor groups get poorer. Globally, this disparity contributes to the gap between the Northern and Southern countries of the world. Within the South, disparities have also sharpened, as a few countries have managed to slow down population growth and raise incomes while others have failed to do so. Poverty in the South has also led to large-scale migration to seek a better life, especially better economic opportunities, in the North. This has created international political frictions. International law and norms make a distinction between migrants (those who voluntarily leave their home countries) and refugees (those who flee from war, natural disaster or political persecution). States are generally supposed to accept refugees, but they do not have to accept migrants. While refugees leave their country of origin, people who have fled their homes but remain within national borders are called 'internally displaced people'. Kashmiri Pandits that fled the violence in the Kashmir Valley in the early 1990s are an example of an internally displaced community. The world refugee map tallies almost perfectly with the world conflicts map because wars and armed conflicts in the South have generated millions of refugees seeking safe haven. From 1990 to 1995, 70 states were involved in 93 wars which killed about 55 lakh people.

❖ Health epidemics such as HIV-AIDS, bird flu, and severe acute respiratory syndrome (SARS) have rapidly spread across countries through migration, business, tourism and military operations. One country's success or failure in limiting the spread of these diseases affects infections in other countries. By 2003, an estimated 4 crore people were infected with HIVAIDS worldwide, two-thirds of them in Africa and half of the rest in South Asia. In North America and other industrialised countries, new drug therapies dramatically lowered the death rate from HIVAIDS in the late 1990s. But these treatments were too expensive to help poor regions like Africa where it has proved to be a major factor in driving the region backward into deeper poverty. Other new and poorly understood diseases such as ebola virus, hantavirus, and hepatitis C have emerged, while old diseases like tuberculosis, malaria, dengue fever and cholera have mutated into drug resistant forms that are difficult to treat. Epidemics among animals have major economic effects. Since the late 1990s, Britain has lost billions of dollars of income during an outbreak of the mad-cow disease, and bird flu shut down supplies of poultry exports from several Asian countries.

❖ **Cooperative Security:** Cooperation may be bilateral (i.e. between any two countries), regional, continental, or global. It would all depend on the nature of the threat and the willingness and ability of countries to respond. Cooperative security may also involve a variety of other players, both international and national—international organisations (the UN, the World Health Organisation, the World Bank, the IMF etc.), non-governmental organizations (Amnesty International, the Red Cross, private foundations and charities, churches and religious organisations, trade unions, associations, social and development organisations), businesses and corporations, and great personalities (e.g. Mother Teresa, Nelson Mandela). Cooperative security may involve the use of force as a last resort.

❖ **India's Security Strategy:** India has faced traditional (military) and non-traditional threats to its security that have emerged from within as well as outside its borders. Its security strategy has four broad components. The first component was strengthening its military capabilities because India has been involved in conflicts with its neighbours —Pakistan in 1947–48, 1965, 1971 and 1999; and China in 1962. Since it is surrounded by nuclear-armed countries in the South Asian region, India's decision to conduct nuclear tests in 1998 was justified by the Indian government in terms of safeguarding national security. India first tested a nuclear device in 1974. The second component of India's security strategy has been to strengthen international norms and international institutions to protect its security interests. India's first Prime Minister, Jawaharlal Nehru, supported the cause of Asian solidarity, decolonisation, disarmament, and the UN as a forum in which international conflicts could be settled. India also took initiatives to bring about a universal and non-discriminatory non-proliferation regime in which all countries would have the same rights and obligations with respect to weapons of mass destruction (nuclear, biological, chemical). It argued for an equitable New International Economic Order (NIEO). Most importantly, it used non-alignment to help carve out an area of peace outside the bloc politics of the two superpowers. India joined 160 countries that have signed and ratified the 1997 Kyoto Protocol, which provides a roadmap for reducing the emissions of greenhouse gases to check global warming. Indian troops have been sent abroad on UN peacekeeping missions in support of cooperative security initiatives. The third component of Indian security strategy is geared towards meeting security challenges within the country. Several militant groups from areas such as the Nagaland, Mizoram, the Punjab, and Kashmir among others have, from time to time, sought to break away from India. India has tried to preserve national unity by adopting a democratic political system, which allows different communities and groups of people to freely articulate their grievances and share political power. Finally, there has been an attempt in India to develop its economy in a way that the vast mass of citizens are lifted out of poverty and misery and huge economic inequalities are not allowed to exist.

Exercise

1. Security policy is concerned with preventing war is called __________.

   (a) Deterrence (b) Defence

   (c) Defend (d) Deny

2. Which of the following Islamic militants group is led by Osama bin Laden?

   (a) Al Laden (b) Al Islamic

   (c) Al Qaeda (d) Al Hibul

3. Biological weapon convention is formed in which of the following year?

   (a) 1960 (b) 1970

   (c) 1971 (d) 1972

4. Consider the following statements about Chemical Weapons Convention:

   i. It banned the production and possession of the weapons.

   ii. 181 states acceded to the CWC.

   Select the correct answer using the code given below:

   (a) i only (b) ii only

   (c) Both (d) Neither

5. The ABM Treaty in 1972 tried to stop the United States and Soviet Union from using ballistic missiles as a defensive shield to launch a nuclear attack. ABM stands for –

   (a) Anti-barring Missile

   (b) Anti-ballistic Missile

   (c) Anti-banned Missile

   (d) Anti-body Missile

6. **Assertion:** Non-traditional views of security have been called 'human security' or 'global security'.

   Reason: Human security is about the protection of people more than the protection of states.

   (a) Both the Assertion and the Reason are correct and the Reason is the correct explanation of the Assertion.

   (b) Both the Assertion and the Reason are correct but the Reason is not the correct explanation of the Assertion.

   (c) The Assertion is incorrect but the Reason is correct.

   (d) The Assertion is correct but the Reason is incorrect.

7. _______________refers to political violence that targets civilians deliberately and indiscriminately.

   (a) Security

   (b) Poverty

   (c) War

   (d) Terrorism

8. India first tested a nuclear device in __________.

   (a) 1974

   (b) 1988

   (c) 1989

   (d) 1975

9. Human rights have come to be classified into three types. Which of the following are the types of human rights?

   i. Political rights

   ii. Economic rights

   iii. Rights of colonised people or ethnic and indigenous minorities

   Select the correct answer using the code given below:

   (a) i and ii only

   (b) ii and iii only

   (c) i and iii only

   (d) i, ii and iii

10. Match the following pairs:

   i.   Confidence Building Measures (CBMs)

   ii. Arms Control

   iii. Alliance

   iv. Disarmament

   (a) Giving up certain types of weapons

   (b) A process of exchanging information on defence matters between nations on a regular basis

   (c) A coalition of nations meant to deter or defend against military attacks

   (d) Regulates the acquisition or development of weapons

Select the correct answer using the code given below:

   (a) (i)-(b); (ii)-(c); (iii)-(d); (iv)-(a)

   (b) (i)-(b); (ii)-(d); (iii)-(c); (iv)-(a)

   (c) (i)-(a); (ii)-(b); (iii)-(c); (iv)-(d)

   (d) (i)-(a); (ii)-(d); (iii)-(c); (iv)-(b)

Answer Keys

1. (a)   2. (c)   3. (d)   4. (c)   5. (b)   6. (b)   7. (d)   8. (a)   9. (d)   10. (b)

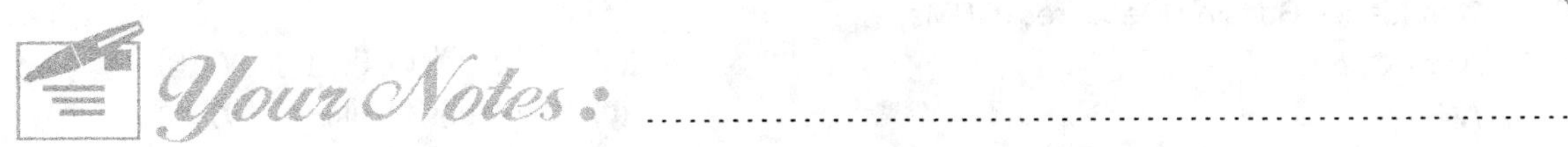
Your Notes :

Environment and Natural Resources

❖ **ENVIRONMENTAL CONCERNS IN GLOBAL POLITICS:** Throughout the world, cultivable area is barely expanding any more, and a substantial portion of existing agricultural land is losing fertility. Grasslands have been overgrazed and fisheries overharvested. Water bodies have suffered extensive depletion and pollution, severely restricting food production. According to the *Human Development Report 2016* of the United Nations Development Programme, 663 million people in developing countries have no access to safe water and 2.4 billion have no access to sanitation, resulting in the death of more than three million children every year. Natural forests — which help stabilise the climate, moderate water supplies, and harbor a majority of the planet's biodiversity on land—are being cut down and people are being displaced. The loss of biodiversity continues due to the destruction of habitat in areas which are rich in species. A steady decline in the total amount of ozone in the Earth's stratosphere (commonly referred to as the ozone hole) poses a real danger to ecosystems and human health. Coastal pollution too is increasing globally. Although the open sea is relatively clean, the coastal waters are becoming increasingly polluted largely due to land-based activities. If unchecked, intensive human settlement of coastal zones across the globe will lead to further deterioration in the quality of marine environment. Although environmental concerns have a long history, awareness of the environmental consequences of economic growth acquired an increasingly political character from the 1960s onwards. The Club of Rome, a global think tank, published a book in 1972 entitled *Limits to Growth*, dramatising the potential depletion of the Earth's resources against the backdrop of rapidly growing world population. International agencies, including the United Nations Environment Programme (UNEP), began holding international conferences and promoting detailed studies to get a more coordinated and effective response to environmental problems. The growing focus on environmental issues within the arena of global politics was firmly consolidated at the United Nations Conference on Environment and Development held in Rio de Janeiro, Brazil, in June 1992. This was also called the Earth Summit. The summit was attended by 170 states, thousands of NGOs and many multinational corporations. Five years earlier, the 1987 Brundtland Report, *Our Common Future*, had warned that traditional patterns of economic growth were not sustainable in the long term, especially in view of the demands of the South for further industrial development. What was obvious at the Rio Summit was that the rich and developed countries of the First World, generally referred to as the 'global North' were pursuing a different environmental agenda than the poor and developing countries of the Third World, called the 'global South'. Whereas the Northern states were concerned with ozone depletion and global warming, the Southern states were anxious to address the relationship between economic development and environmental management. The Rio Summit produced conventions dealing with climate change, biodiversity, forestry, and recommended a list of development practices called 'Agenda 21'. But it left unresolved considerable differences and difficulties. There was a consensus on combining economic growth with ecological responsibility. This approach to development is commonly known as 'sustainable development'.

❖ **THE PROTECTION OF GLOBAL COMMONS:** 'Commons' are those resources which are not owned by anyone but rather shared by a community. Similarly, there are some areas or regions of the world which are located outside the sovereign jurisdiction of any one state, and therefore require common governance by the international community. These are known as *res communis humanitatis* or *global commons.* They include the earth's atmosphere, Antarctica, the ocean floor, and outer space. Cooperation over the global commons is not easy. There have been many path-breaking agreements such as the 1959 Antarctic Treaty, the 1987 Montreal Protocol, and the 1991 Antarctic Environmental Protocol. A major problem underlying all ecological issues relates to the difficulty of achieving consensus on common environmental agendas on the basis of vague scientific evidence and time frames. In that sense the discovery of the ozone hole over the Antarctic in the mid-1980s revealed the opportunity as well as dangers inherent in tackling global environmental problems.

❖ **COMMON BUT DIFFERENTIATED RESPONSIBILITIES:** The developed countries of the North want to discuss the environmental issue as it stands now and want everyone to be equally responsible for ecological conservation. The developing countries of the South feel that much of the ecological degradation in the world is the product of industrial development undertaken by the developed countries. If they have caused more degradation, they must also take more responsibility for undoing the damage now. Moreover, the developing countries are in the process of industrialization and they must not be subjected to the same restrictions, which apply to the developed countries. Thus the special needs of the developing countries must be taken into account in the development, application, and interpretation of rules of international environmental law. This argument was accepted in the Rio Declaration at the Earth Summit in 1992 and is called the principle of 'common but differentiated responsibilities'. The relevant part of the Rio Declaration says that "States shall cooperate in the spirit of global partnership to conserve, protect and restore the health and integrity of the Earth's ecosystem. In view of the different contributions of global environmental degradation, states have common but differentiated responsibilities. The developed countries acknowledge the responsibility that they bear in the international pursuit of sustainable development in view of the pressures their societies place on the global environment and of the technological and financial resources they command." The 1992 United Nations Framework Convention on Climate Change (UNFCCC) also provides that the parties should act to protect the climate system "on the basis of equity and in accordance with their common but differentiated responsibilities and respective capabilities." The parties to the Convention agreed that the largest share of historical and current global emissions of greenhouse gases has originated in developed countries. It was also acknowledged that per capita emissions in developing countries are still relatively low. China, India, and other developing countries were, therefore, exempted from the requirements of the Kyoto Protocol. The Kyoto Protocol is an international agreement setting targets for industrialised countries to cut their greenhouse gas emissions. Certain gases like Carbon dioxide, Methane, Hydro-fluoro carbons etc. are considered at least partly responsible for global warming - the rise in global temperature which may have catastrophic consequences for life on Earth. The protocol was agreed to in 1997 in Kyoto in Japan, based on principles set out in UNFCCC.

❖ **COMMON PROPERTY RESOURCES:** Common property represents common property for the group. The underlying norm here is that members of the group have both rights and duties with respect to the nature, levels of use, and the maintenance of a given resource. Through mutual understanding and centuries of practice, many village communities in India, for example, have defined members' rights and responsibilities. A combination of factors, including privatisation, agricultural intensification, population growth and ecosystem degradation have caused common property to dwindle in size, quality, and availability to the poor in much of the world. The institutional arrangement for the actual management of the sacred groves on state-owned forest land appropriately fits the description of a common property regime. Along the forest belt of South India, sacred groves have been traditionally managed by village communities.

❖ **INDIA'S STAND ON ENVIRONMENTAL ISSUES:** India signed and ratified the 1997 Kyoto Protocol in August 2002. India, China and other developing countries were exempt from the requirements of the Kyoto Protocol because their contribution to the emission of greenhouse gases during the industrialisation period (that is believed to be causing today's global warming and climate change) was not significant. However, the critics of the Kyoto Protocol point out that sooner or later, both India and China, along with other developing countries, will be among the leading countributors to greenhouse gas emissions. At the G-8 meeting in June 2005, India pointed out that the per capita emission rates of the developing countries are a tiny fraction of those in the developed world. Following the principle of common but differentiated responsibilities, India is of the view that the major responsibility of curbing emission rests with the developed countries, which have accumulated emissions over a long period of time. India's international negotiating position relies heavily on principles of historical responsibility, as enshrined in UNFCCC. This acknowledges that developed countries are responsible for most historical and current greenhouse gas emissions, and emphasizes that 'economic and social development are the first and overriding priorities of the developing country parties'. So India is wary of recent discussions within UNFCCC about introducing binding commitments on rapidly industrialising countries (such as Brazil, China and India) to reduce their greenhouse gas emissions. India feels this contravenes the very spirit of UNFCCC. Neither does it seem fair to impose restrictions on India when the country's rise in per capita carbon emissions by 2030 is likely to still represent less than half the world average of 3.8 tonnes in 2000. Indian emissions are predicted to rise from 0.9 tonnes per capita in 2000 to 1.6 tonnes per capita in 2030. The Indian government is already participating in global efforts through a number of programmes. For example, India's National Auto-fuel Policy mandates cleaner fuels for vehicles. The Energy Conservation Act, passed in 2001, outlines initiatives to improve energy efficiency. Similarly, the Electricity Act of 2003 encourages the use of renewable energy. Recent trends in importing natural gas and encouraging the adoption of clean coal technologies show that India has been making real efforts. The government is also keen to launch a National Mission on Biodiesel, using about 11 million hectares of land to produce biodiesel by 2011–2012. India ratified the Paris Climate Agreement on 2 October 2016. And India has one of the largest renewable energy programmes in the world. A review of the implementation of the agreements at the Earth Summit in Rio was undertaken by India in 1997. One of the key conclusions was that there had been no meaningful progress with respect to transfer of new and additional financial resources and environmentally-sound technology on concessional terms to developing nations. India finds it necessary that developed countries take immediate measures to provide developing countries with financial resources and clean technologies to enable them to meet their existing commitments under UNFCCC. India is also of the view that the SAARC countries should adopt a common position on major global environment issues, so that the region's voice carries greater weight.

❖ **ENVIRONMENTAL MOVEMENTS: ONE OR MANY?** The forest movements of the South, in Mexico, Chile, Brazil, Malaysia, Indonesia, continental Africa and India (just to list a few examples) are faced with enormous pressures. Forest clearing in the Third World continues at an alarming rate, despite three decades of environmental activism. The destruction of the world's last remaining grand forests has actually increased in the last decade. The minerals industry is one of the most powerful forms of industry on the planet. A large number of economies of the South are now being re-opened to MNCs through the liberalisation of the global economy. The mineral industry's extraction of earth, its use of chemicals, its pollution of waterways and land, its clearance of native vegetation, its displacement of communities, amongst other factors, continue to invite criticism and resistance in various parts of the globe. One good example is that of the Philippines, where a vast network of groups and organizations campaigned against the Western Mining Corporation (WMC), and an Australia-based multinational company. Much opposition to the company in its own country, Australia, is based on anti-nuclear sentiments and advocacy for the basic rights of Australian indigenous peoples. Another group of movements are those involved in struggles against mega-dams. In every country where a mega-dam is being built, one is likely to find an environmental movement opposing it. Increasingly anti-dam movements are pro-river movements for more sustainable and equitable management of river systems and valleys. The early 1980s saw the first anti-dam movement launched in the North, namely, the campaign to save the Franklin River and its surrounding forests in Australia. This was a wilderness and forest campaign as well as anti-dam campaign. At present, there has been a spurt in mega-dam building in the South, from Turkey to Thailand to South Africa, from Indonesia to China. India has had some of the leading anti-dam, pro-river movements. Narmada Bachao Andolan is one of the best known of these movements. It is significant to note that, in anti-dam and other environmental movements in India, the most important shared idea is non-violence.

❖ **RESOURCE GEOPOLITICS:** Resource geopolitics is all about who gets what, when, where and how. Resources have provided some of the key means and motives of global European power expansion. They have also been the focus of inter-state rivalry. Western geopolitical thinking about resources has been dominated by the relationship of trade, war and power, at the core of which were overseas resources and maritime navigation. Since sea power itself rested on access to timber, naval timber supply became a key priority for major European powers from the 17th century onwards. The critical importance of ensuring uninterrupted supply of strategic resources, in particular oil, was well established both during the First World War and the Second World War. Throughout the Cold War the industrialised countries of the North adopted a number of methods to ensure a steady flow of resources. These included the deployment of military forces near exploitation sites and along sealanes of communication, the stockpiling of strategic resources, efforts to prop up friendly governments in producing countries, as well as support to multinational companies and favourable international agreements. Traditional Western strategic thinking remained concerned with access to supplies, which might be threatened by the Soviet Union. A particular concern was Western control of oil in the Gulf and strategic minerals in Southern and Central Africa. After the end of the Cold War and the disintegration of the Soviet Union, the security of supply continues to worry government and business decisions with regard to several minerals, in particular radioactive materials. However, oil continues to be the most important resource in global strategy. The global economy relied on oil for much of the 20th century as a portable and indispensable fuel. The immense wealth associated with oil generates political struggles to control it, and the history of petroleum is also the history of war and struggle. Nowhere is this more obviously the case than in West Asia and Central Asia. West Asia, specifically the Gulf region, accounts for about 30 per cent of global oil production. But it has about 64 percent of the planet's known reserves, and is therefore the only region able to satisfy any substantial rise in oil demand. Saudi Arabia has a quarter of the world's total reserves and is the single largest producer. Iraq's known reserves are second only to Saudi Arabia's. And, since substantial portions of Iraqi territory are yet to be fully explored, there is a fair chance that actual reserves might be far larger. The United States, Europe, Japan, and increasingly India and China, which consume this petroleum, are located at a considerable distance from the region. Water is another crucial resource that is relevant to global politics. Regional variations and the increasing scarcity of freshwater in some parts of the world point to the possibility of disagreements over shared water resources as a leading source of conflicts in the 21st century. Some commentators on world politics have referred to 'water wars' to describe the possibility of violent conflict over this life sustaining resource. Countries that share rivers can disagree over many things. For instance, a typical disagreement is a downstream (lower riparian) state's objection to pollution, excessive irrigation, or the construction of dams by an upstream (upper riparian) state, which might decrease or degrade the quality of water available to the downstream state. States have used force to protect or seize freshwater resources. Examples of violence include those between Israel, Syria, and Jordan in the 1950s and 1960s over attempts by each side to divert water from the Jordan and Yarmuk Rivers, and more recent threats between Turkey, Syria, and Iraq over the construction of dams on the Euphrates River. A number of studies show that countries that share rivers — and many countries do share rivers — are involved in military conflicts with each other.

❖ **THE INDIGENOUS PEOPLES AND THEIR RIGHTS:** The question of indigenous people brings the issues of environment, resources and politics together. The UN defines indigenous populations as comprising the descendants of peoples who inhabited the present territory of a country at the time when persons of a different culture or ethnic origin arrived there from other parts of the world and overcame them. Indigenous people today live more in conformity with their particular social, economic, and cultural customs and traditions than the institutions of the country of which they now form a part. Approximately 30 crore indigenous peoples spread throughout the world including India. There are 20 lakh indigenous people of the Cordillera region of the Philippines, 10 lakh Mapuche people of Chile, six lakh tribal people of the Chittagong Hill Tracts in Bangladesh, 35 lakh North American natives, 50,000 Kuna living east of Panama Canal and 10 lakh Small Peoples of the Soviet North. Like other social movements, indigenous people speak of their struggles, their agenda and their rights. Indigenous people occupy areas in Central and South America, Africa, India (where they are known as Tribals) and Southeast Asia. Many of the present day island states in the Oceania region (including Australia and New Zealand), were inhabited by the Polynesian, Melanesian and Micronesian people over the course of thousands of years. They appeal to governments to come to terms with the continuing existence of indigenous nations as enduring communities with an identity of their own. In India, the description 'indigenous people' is usually applied to the Scheduled Tribes who constitute nearly eight per cent of the population of the country. With the exception of small communities of hunters and gatherers, most indigenous populations in India depend for their subsistence primarily on the cultivation of land. For centuries, if not millennia, they had free access to as much land as they could cultivate. It was only after the establishment of the British colonial rule that areas, which had previously been inhabited by the Scheduled Tribe communities, were subjected to outside forces. Although they enjoy a constitutional protection in political representation, they have not got much of the benefits of development in the country. In fact they have paid a huge cost for development since they are the single largest group among the people displaced by various developmental projects since independence. The World Council of Indigenous Peoples was formed in 1975. The Council became subsequently the first of 11 indigenous NGOs to receive consultative status in the UN.

Exercise

1. Human Development Report is published by which of the following organization?
   (a) United Nations Development Programme
   (b) World Health Organisation
   (c) Intenational Monetary Fund
   (d) World Bank

2. A steady decline in the total amount of ozone in the Earth's stratosphere commonly referred to as the _____.
   (a) Ozone decline
   (b) Ozone degradation
   (c) Ozone hole
   (d) Ozone depletion

3. Which the following statements are Not correct about the Earth Summit?
   i. It was attended by 170 countries, thousands of NGOs and many MNCs.
   ii. The summit was held under the aegis of the UN.
   iii. For the first time, global environmental issues were firmly consolidated at the political level.
   iv. It was a summit meeting.
   Select the correct answer using the code given below:
   (a) i and iii only　　　(b) ii and iv only
   (c) ii and iii only　　　(d) i and iv only

4. Which of the following statement is correct about the global commons?
   (a) The Earth's atmosphere, Antarctica, ocean floor and outer space are considered as part of the global commons.
   (b) The global commons are outside sovereign jurisdiction.
   (c) The question of managing the global commons has reflected the North-South divide.
   (d) The countries of the North are more concerned about the protection of the global commons than the countries of the South.

5. What were the outcomes of Rio-Summit?
   i. Rio-Summit produced conventions dealing with climate change, biodiversity, forestry and recommended a list of development practices called Agenda 21.
   ii. It gave the concept of sustainable development to be combined economic growth with ecological responsibility.
   iii. Rio-Summit developed various contentious issues like Commons, Global Commons in global politics of environment.
   Select the correct answer using the code given below:
   (a) i and ii only　　　(b) ii and iii only
   (c) i and iii only　　　(d) i, ii and iii

6. Some areas or regions of the world which are located outside the sovereign jurisdiction of any one state, and therefore require common governance by the international community. These are known as _________ or _______.
   (a) res communis humanitatis, global commons
   (b) commons, global commons
   (c) res community, global commons
   (d) res humanitatis, commons

7. The Rio-Summit held in which of the following year?
   (a) 1991　　　　　　(b) 1992
   (c) 1993　　　　　　(d) 1994

8. **Assertion:** The Kyoto Protocol is an international agreement setting targets for industrialised countries to cut their greenhouse gas emissions.
   Reasons: The protocol was agreed to in 1997 in Kyoto in Japan, based on principles set out in UNFCCC.
   (a) Both the Assertion and the Reason are correct and the Reason is the correct explanation of the Assertion.
   (b) Both the Assertion and the Reason are correct but the Reason is not the correct explanation of the Assertion.
   (c) The Assertion is incorrect but the Reason is correct.
   (d) The Assertion is correct but the Reason is incorrect.

9. Common but _________ responsibilities mean that the state shall cooperate in the spirit of global partnership to conserve, protect and restore the health and integrity of the earth's ecosystem.
   (a) Common　　　　(b) Cooperative
   (c) Differentiated　　(d) Different

10. The World Council of Indigenous Peoples was formed in _____.
    (a) 1970　　　　　　(b) 1973
    (c) 1974　　　　　　(d) 1975

Answer Keys

1. (a)　　2. (c)　　3. (b)　　4. (a)　　5. (d)　　6. (a)　　7. (b)　　8. (b)　　9. (c)　　10. (d)

CHAPTER 9

Globalisation

- ❖ Globalisation need not always be positive; it can have negative consequences for the people.

- ❖ Globalisation as a concept fundamentally deals with flows. These flows could be of various kinds — ideas moving from one part of the world to another, capital shunted between two or more places, commodities being traded across borders, and people moving in search of better livelihoods to different parts of the world. The crucial element is the 'worldwide interconnectedness' that is created and sustained as a consequence of these constant flows.

- ❖ Globalisation is a multidimensional concept. It has political, economic and cultural manifestations.

- ❖ The impact of globalisation is vastly uneven — it affects some societies more than others and some parts of some societies more than others.

- ❖ **CAUSES OF GLOBALISATION:** While globalisation is not caused by any single factor, technology remains a critical element. There is no doubt that the invention of the telegraph, the telephone, and the microchip in more recent times has revolutionised communication between different parts of the world.

- ❖ **POLITICAL CONSEQUENCES:** Globalisation results in an erosion of state capacity, that is, the ability of government to do what they do. All over the world, the old 'welfare state' is now giving way to a more minimalist state that performs certain core functions such as the maintenance of law and order and the security of its citizens. However, it withdraws from many of its earlier welfare functions directed at economic and social well-being. In place of the welfare state, it is the market that becomes the prime determinant of economic and social priorities. The entry and the increased role of multinational companies all over the world lead to a reduction in the capacity of governments to take decisions on their own. State capacity has received a boost as a consequence of globalisation, with enhanced technologies available at the disposal of the state to collect information about its citizens. With this information, the state is better able to rule, not less able. Thus, states become more powerful than they were earlier as an outcome of the new technology.

- ❖ **ECONOMIC CONSEQUENCES:** Economic globalisation draws our attention immediately to the role of international institutions like the IMF and the WTO and the role they play in determining economic policies across the world. Economic globalisation usually involves greater economic flows among different countries of the world. Some of this is voluntary and some forced by international institutions and powerful countries. Globalisation has involved greater trade in commodities across the globe; the restrictions imposed by different countries on allowing the imports of other countries have been reduced. Similarly, the restrictions on movement of capital across countries have also been reduced. In operational terms, it means that investors in the rich countries can invest their money in countries other than their own, including developing countries, where they might get better returns. Globalisation has also led to the flow of ideas across national boundaries. The spread of internet and computer related services are an example of that. But globalisation has not led to the same degree of increase in the movement of people across the globe. Developed countries have carefully guarded their borders with visa policies to ensure that citizens of other countries cannot take away the jobs of their own citizens. Globalisation has led to similar economic policies adopted by governments in different parts of the world, this has generated vastly different outcomes in different parts of the world. Economic globalisation has created an intense division of opinion all over the world. Those who are concerned about social justice are worried about the extent of state withdrawal caused by processes of economic globalisation. They point out that it is likely to benefit only a small section of the population while impoverishing those who were dependent on the government for jobs and welfare (education, health, sanitation, etc.). They have emphasised the need to ensure institutional safeguards or creating 'social safety nets' to minimise the negative effects of globalisation on those who are economically weak. Many movements all over the world feel that safety nets are insufficient or unworkable. They have called for a halt to forced economic globalisation, for its results would lead to economic ruin for the weaker countries, especially for the poor within these countries. Some economists have described economic globalisation as recolonisation of the world. Increased momentum towards inter - dependence and integration between governments, businesses, and ordinary people in different parts of the world as a result of globalisation.

❖ **CULTURAL CONSEQUENCES:** The cultural effect of globalisation leads to the fear that this process poses a threat to cultures in the world. It does so, because globalisation leads to the rise of a uniform culture or what is called cultural homogenisation. The rise of a uniform culture is not the emergence of a global culture. What we have in the name of a global culture is the imposition of Western culture on the rest of the world. While cultural homogenization is an aspect of globalisation, the same process also generates precisely the opposite effect. It leads to each culture becoming more different and distinctive. This phenomenon is called cultural heterogenisation.

❖ **INDIA AND GLOBALISATION:** During the colonial period, as a consequence of Britain's imperial ambitions, India became an exporter of primary goods and raw materials and a consumer of finished goods. After independence, because of this experience with the British, we decided to make things ourselves rather than relying on others. We also decided not to allow others to export to us so that our own producers could learn to make things. This 'protectionism' generated its own problems. While some advances were made in certain arenas, critical sectors such as health, housing and primary education did not receive the attention they

deserved. India had a fairly sluggish rate of economic growth. In 1991, responding to a financial crisis and to the desire for higher rates of economic growth, India embarked on a programme of economic reforms that has sought increasingly to de-regulate various sectors including trade and foreign investment.

❖ **RESISTANCE TO GLOBALISATION:** Critics of globalisation make a variety of arguments. Those on the left argue that contemporary globalisation represents a particular phase of global capitalism that makes the rich richer (and fewer) and the poor poorer. Weakening of the state leads to a reduction in the capacity of the state to protect the interest of its poor. Critics of globalisation from the political right express anxiety over the political, economic and cultural effects. In political terms, they also fear the weakening of the state. Economically, they want a return to self-reliance and protectionism, at least in certain areas of the economy. Culturally, they are worried that traditional culture will be harmed and people will lose their age-old values and ways. Many anti-globalisation movements are not opposed to the idea of globalisation *per se* as much as they are opposed to a specific programme of globalisation, which they see as a form of imperialism. In 1999, at the World Trade Organisation (WTO) Ministerial Meeting there were widespread protests at Seattle alleging unfair trading practices by the economically powerful states. It was argued that the interests of the developing world were not given sufficient importance in the evolving global economic system. The World Social Forum (WSF) is another global platform, which brings together a wide coalition composed of human rights activists, environmentalists, labour, youth and women activists opposed to neo-liberal globalisation. The first WSF meeting was organised in Porto Alegre, Brazil in 2001. The fourth WSF meeting was held in Mumbai in 2004. The latest WSF meeting was held in Brazil in March 2018.

❖ **INDIA AND RESISTANCE TO GLOBALISATION:** Resistance to globalisation in India has come from different quarters. There have been left wing protests to economic liberalisation voiced through political parties as well as through forums like the Indian Social Forum. Trade unions of industrial workforce as well as those representing farmer interests have organised protests against the entry of multinationals. The patenting of certain plants like *Neem* by American and European firms has also generated considerable opposition.

Exercise

1. **Assertion:** Globalisation is a one way.

   Reason: Globalisation need not always be positive; it can have negative consequences for the people.

   (a) Both the Assertion and the Reason are correct and the Reason is the correct explanation of the Assertion.

   (b) Both the Assertion and the Reason are correct but the Reason is not the correct explanation of the Assertion.

   (c) The Assertion is incorrect but the Reason is correct.

   (d) The Assertion is correct but the Reason is incorrect.

2. **Assertion:** Globalisation is a multidimensional concept.

   Reason: It has political, economic and cultural manifestations.

   (a) Both the Assertion and the Reason are correct and the Reason is the correct explanation of the Assertion.

   (b) Both the Assertion and the Reason are correct but the Reason is not the correct explanation of the Assertion.

   (c) The Assertion is incorrect but the Reason is correct.

   (d) The Assertion is correct but the Reason is incorrect.

3. **Assertion:** While cultural homogenization is an aspect of globalisation, the same process also generates precisely the opposite effect.

   Reason: It leads to each culture becoming more different and distinctive. This phenomenon is called cultural heterogenisation.

   (a) Both the Assertion and the Reason are correct and the Reason is the correct explanation of the Assertion.

   (b) Both the Assertion and the Reason are correct but the Reason is not the correct explanation of the Assertion.

   (c) The Assertion is incorrect but the Reason is correct.

   (d) The Assertion is correct but the Reason is incorrect.

4. Globalisation is a multi dimensional concept. It includes which of the following manifestations?

   i.   Political

   ii. Economic

   iii. Cultural

   iv. Social

   Select the correct answer using the code given below:

   (a) i and ii only

   (b) ii and iv only

   (c) i, ii and iii only

   (d) i, ii, iii and iv

5. The cultural effect of globalisation leads to the fear that this process poses a threat to cultures in the world. It does so, because globalisation leads to the rise of a uniform culture or what is called cultural _________.

   (a) Homogenization

   (b) Hetronisation

   (c) Homogeneity

   (d) Heterogeneity

6. Globalisation in India started in the year ______.

   (a) 1990

   (b) 1991

   (c) 1992

   (d) 1993

7. Which of the statements is incorrect about globalisation?

   i.   Advocates of globalisation argue that it will result in greater economic growth.

   ii. Critics of globalisation argue that it will result in greater economic disparity.

   iii. Advocates of globalisation argue that it will result in cultural homogenisation.

   iv. Critics of globalisation argue that it will result in cultural homogenisation.

   Select the correct answer using the code given below:

   (a) i and iii only

   (b) i and iv only

   (c) ii and iii only

   (d) ii and iv only

8. Which of the statement is correct about the impact of globalisation?

    (a) Globalisation is even in its impact on states and societies.

    (b) Globalisation has had a uniform impact on all states and societies.

    (c) The impact of globalisation has been confined to the political sphere.

    (d) Globalisation inevitably results in cultural homogeneity.

9. Which of the statement is correct about the causes of globalisation?

    (a) Technology is not an important cause of globalisation.

    (b) Globalisation is caused by a particular community of people.

    (c) Globalisation originated in the US.

    (d) Economic interdependence alone causes globalisation.

10. Which of the statements are TRUE about globalisation?

    (a) Globalisation is only about movement of commodities

    (b) Globalisation does not involve a conflict of values.

    (c) Services are an insignificant part of globalisation.

    (d) Globalisation is about limited interconnectedness.

Answer Keys

1. (d)   2. (a)   3. (a)   4. (c)   5. (a)   6. (b)   7. (d)   8. (b)   9. (c)   10. (b)

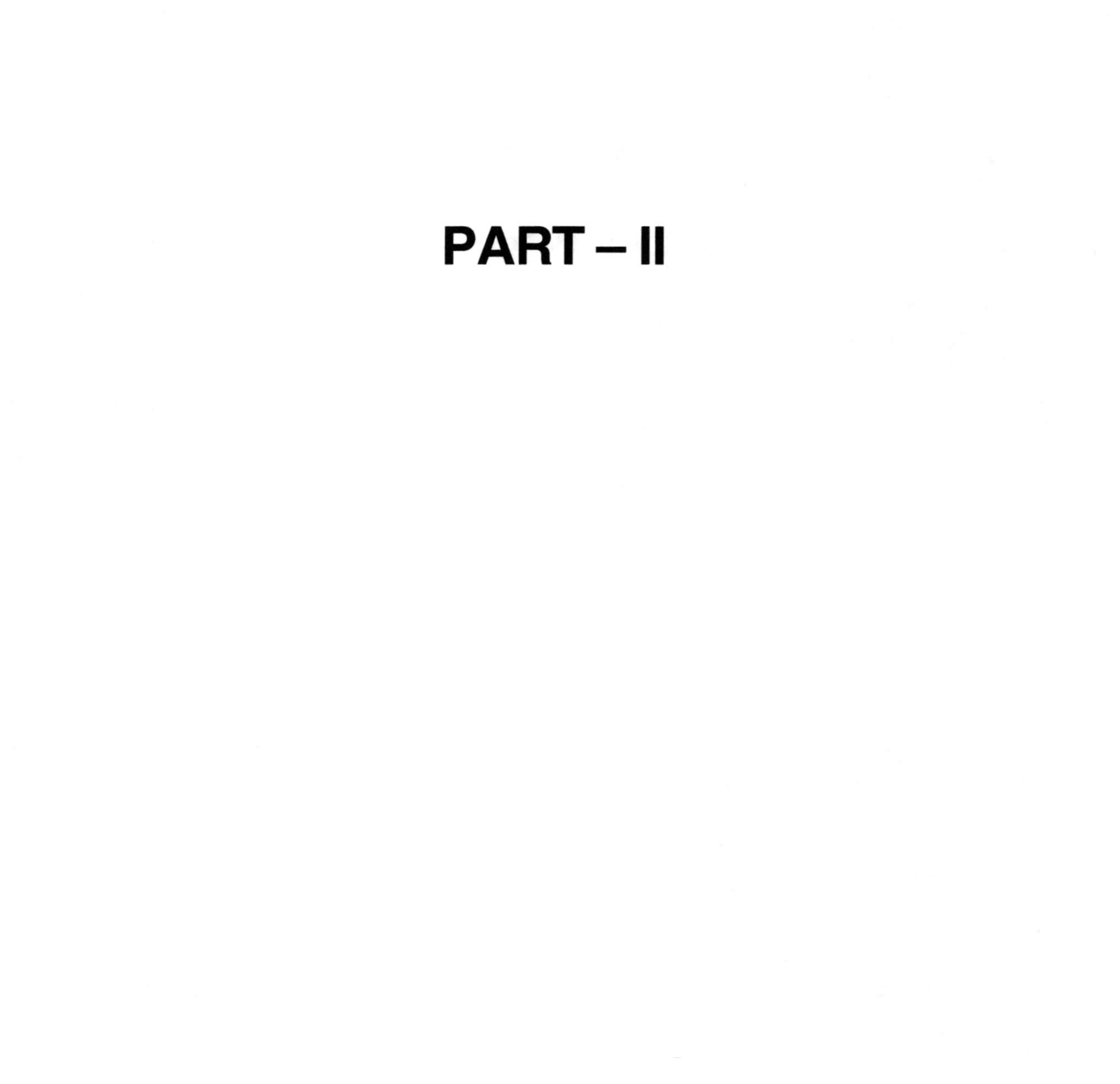

PART – II

Challenges of Nation Building

- ❖ At the hour of midnight on 14-15 August 1947, India attained independence. Jawaharlal Nehru, the first prime minister of free India, addressed a special session of the Constituent Assembly that night. This was the famous 'tryst with destiny' speech.

- ❖ There were two goals almost everyone agreed upon: one, that after independence, we shall run our country through democratic government; and two, that the government will be run for the good of all, particularly the poor and the socially disadvantaged groups.

- ❖ Three Challenges - The first and the immediate challenge was to shape a nation that was united, yet accommodative of the diversity in our society. India was a land of continental size and diversity. Its people spoke different languages and followed different cultures and religions. The second challenge was to establish democracy. The Constitution granted fundamental rights and extended the right to vote to every citizen. India adopted representative democracy based on the parliamentary form of government. A democratic constitution is necessary but not sufficient for establishing a democracy. The challenge was to develop democratic practices in accordance with the Constitution. The third challenge was to ensure the development and wellbeing of the entire society and not only of some sections. Here again the Constitution clearly laid down the principle of equality and special protection to socially disadvantaged groups and religious and cultural communities. The Constitution also set out in the Directive Principles of State Policy the welfare goals that democratic politics must achieve. The real challenge now was to evolve effective policies for economic development and eradication of poverty.

- ❖ On 14-15 August 1947, not one but two nation-states came into existence. India and Pakistan. This was a result of 'partition', the division of British India into India and Pakistan. According to the 'two-nation theory' advanced by the Muslim League, India consisted of not one but two 'people', Hindus and Muslims. That is why it demanded Pakistan, a separate country for the Muslims. The Congress opposed this theory and the demand for Pakistan.

- ❖ Process of Partition - It was decided to follow the principle of religious majorities. This basically means that areas where the Muslims were in majority would make up the territory of Pakistan. There was no single belt of Muslim majority areas in British India. There were two areas of concentration, one in the west and one in the east. There was no way these two parts could be joined. So it was decided that the new country, Pakistan, will comprise two territories, West and East Pakistan separated by a long expanse of Indian Territory. Not all Muslim majority areas wanted to be in Pakistan. Khan Abdul Gaffar Khan, the undisputed leader of the North Western Frontier Province and known as 'Frontier Gandhi', was staunchly opposed to the two-nation theory. Eventually, his voice was simply ignored and the NWFP was made to merge with Pakistan. The third problem was that two of the Muslim majority provinces of British India, Punjab and Bengal, had very large areas where the non-Muslims were in majority. Eventually it was decided that these two provinces would be bifurcated according to the religious majority at the district or even lower level. This decision could not be made by the midnight of 14-15 August. It meant that a large number of people did not know on the day of Independence whether they were in India or in Pakistan. Fourth was the problem of 'minorities' on both sides of the border. Lakhs of Hindus and Sikhs in the areas that were now in Pakistan and an equally large number of Muslims on the Indian side of Punjab and Bengal (and to some extent Delhi and surrounding areas) found themselves trapped.

❖ Consequences of Partition - The year 1947 was the year of one of the largest, most abrupt, unplanned and tragic transfer of population that human history has known. There were killings and atrocities on both sides of the border. In the name of religion people of one community ruthlessly killed and maimed people of the other community. Cities like Lahore, Amritsar and Kolkata became divided into 'communal zones'. Muslims would avoid going into an area where mainly Hindus or Sikhs lived; similarly the Hindus and Sikhs stayed away from areas of Muslim predominance. Forced to abandon their homes and move across borders, people went through immense sufferings. Minorities on both sides of the border fled their home and often secured temporary shelter in 'refugee camps'. Even during this journey they were often attacked, killed or raped. Thousands of women were abducted on both sides of the border. They were made to convert to the religion of the abductor and were forced into marriage. In many cases women were killed by their own family members to preserve the 'family honour'. Many children were separated from their parents. It is estimated that the Partition forced about 80 lakh people to migrate across the new border. Between five to ten lakh people were killed in Partition related violence.

❖ On 30 January 1948, one such extremist, Nathuram Vinayak Godse, walked up to Gandhi ji during his evening prayer in Delhi and fired three bullets at him, killing him instantly. Thus ended a life long struggle for truth, non-violence, justice and tolerance.

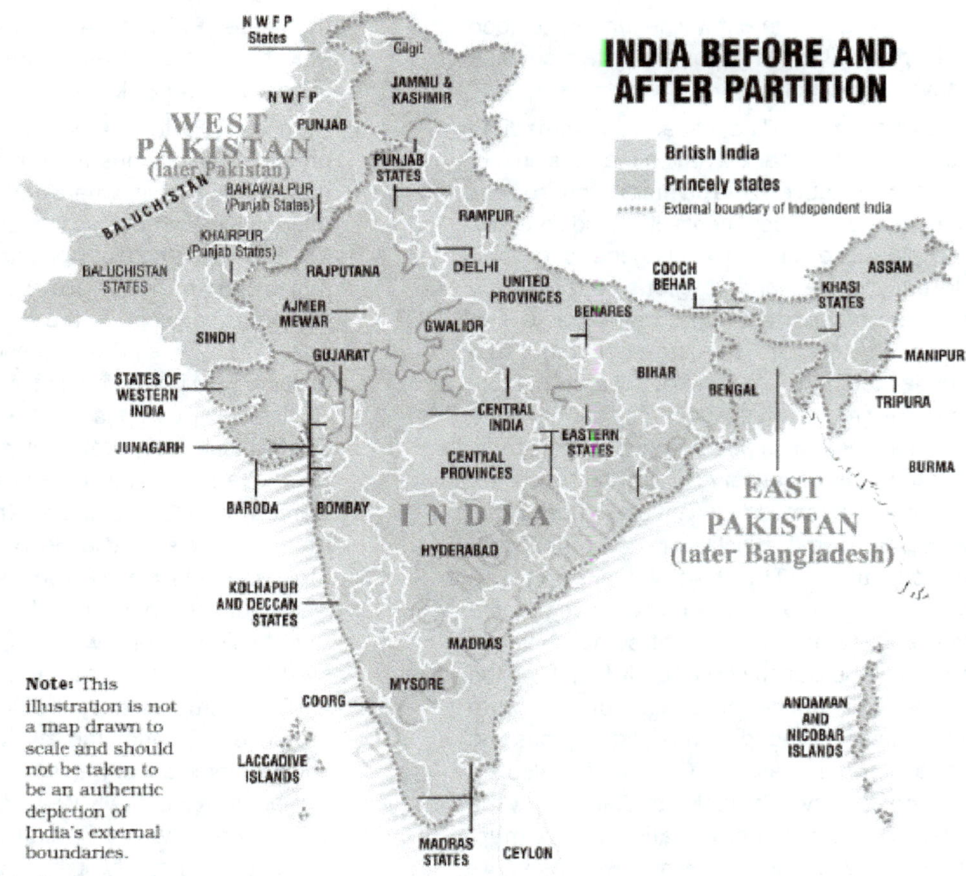

❖ British India was divided into what were called the British Indian Provinces and the Princely States. The British Indian Provinces were directly under the control of the British government. On the other hand, several large and small states ruled by princes, called the Princely States, enjoyed some form of control over their internal affairs as long as they accepted British supremacy. This was called paramountcy or suzerainty of the British crown. Princely States covered one-third of the land area of the British Indian Empire and one out of four Indians lived under princely rule. Just before Independence it was announced by the British that with the end of their rule over India, paramountcy of the British crown over Princely States would also lapse. This meant that all these states, as many as 565 in all, would become legally independent. The British government took the view that all these states were free to join either India or Pakistan or remain independent if they so wished. This decision was left not to the people but to the princely rulers of these states. First of all, the ruler of Travancore announced that the state had decided on Independence. The Nizam of Hyderabad made a similar announcement the next day. Rulers like the Nawab of Bhopal were averse to joining the Constituent Assembly.

❖ The government's approach was guided by three considerations. Firstly, the people of most of the princely states clearly wanted to become part of the Indian union. Secondly, the government was prepared to be flexible in giving autonomy to some regions. The idea was to accommodate plurality and adopt a flexible approach in dealing with the demands of the regions. Thirdly, in the backdrop of Partition which brought into focus the contest over demarcation of territory, the integration and consolidation of the territorial boundaries of the nation had assumed supreme importance.

❖ Before 15 August 1947, peaceful negotiations had brought almost all states whose territories were contiguous to the new boundaries of India, into the Indian Union. The rulers of most of the states signed a document called the 'Instrument of Accession' which meant that their state agreed to become a part of the Union of India. Accession of the Princely States of Junagadh, Hyderabad, Kashmir and Manipur proved more difficult than the rest. The issue of Junagarh was resolved after a plebiscite confirmed people's desire to join India.

❖ Hyderabad - Hyderabad, the largest of the Princely States was surrounded entirely by Indian Territory. Some parts of the old Hyderabad state are today parts of Maharashtra, Karnataka and Andhra Pradesh. Its ruler carried the title, 'Nizam', and he was one of the world's richest men. The Nizam wanted an independent status for Hyderabad. He entered into what was called the Standstill Agreement with India in November 1947 for a year while negotiations with the Indian government were going on. In the meantime, a movement of the people of Hyderabad State against the Nizam's rule gathered force. The peasantry in the Telangana region in particular, was the victim of Nizam's oppressive rule and rose against him. Women who had seen the worst of this oppression joined the movement in large numbers. Hyderabad town was the nerve centre of this movement. The Communists and the Hyderabad Congress were in the forefront of the movement. The Nizam responded by unleashing a para-military force known as the Razakars on the people. The atrocities and communal nature of the Razakars knew no bounds. They murdered, maimed, raped and looted, targeting particularly the non-Muslims. The central government had to order the army to tackle the situation. In September 1948, Indian army moved in to control the Nizam's forces. After a few days of intermittent fighting, the Nizam surrendered. This led to Hyderabad's accession to India.

❖ Manipur - A few days before Independence, the Maharaja of Manipur, Bodhachandra Singh, signed the Instrument of Accession with the Indian government on the assurance that the internal autonomy of Manipur would be maintained. Under the pressure of public opinion, the Maharaja held elections in Manipur in June 1948 and the state became a constitutional monarchy. Thus Manipur was the first part of India to hold an election based on universal adult franchise. In the Legislative Assembly of Manipur there were sharp differences over the question of merger of Manipur with India. While the state Congress wanted the merger, other political parties were opposed to this. The Government of India succeeded in pressurizing the Maharaja into signing a Merger Agreement in September 1949, without consulting the popularly elected Legislative Assembly of Manipur.

❖ During colonial rule, the state boundaries were drawn either on administrative convenience or simply coincided with the territories annexed by the British government or the territories ruled by the princely powers.

❖ Our national movement had rejected these divisions as artificial and had promised the linguistic principle as the basis of formation of states. In fact after the Nagpur session of Congress in 1920 the principle was recognised as the basis of the reorganisation of the Indian National Congress party itself. Many Provincial Congress Committees were created by linguistic zones, which did not follow the administrative divisions of British India.

❖ Things changed after Independence and Partition. Our leaders felt that carving out states on the basis of language might lead to disruption and disintegration. This decision of the national leadership was challenged by the local leaders and the people. Protests began in the Telugu speaking areas of the old Madras province, which included present day Tamil Nadu, parts of Andhra Pradesh, Kerala and Karnataka. The Vishalandhra movement (as the movement for a separate Andhra was called) demanded that the Telugu speaking areas should be separated from the Madras province of which they were a part and be made into a separate Andhra province. Nearly all the political forces in the Andhra region were in favour of linguistic reorganisation of the then Madras province. The movement gathered momentum as a result of the Central government's vacillation. Potti Sriramulu, a Congress leader and a veteran Gandhian, went on an indefinite fast that led to his death after 56 days. This caused great unrest and resulted in violent outbursts in Andhra region. People in large numbers took to the streets. Many were injured or lost their lives in police firing. In Madras, several legislators resigned their seats in protest. Finally, the Prime Minister announced the formation of a separate Andhra state in December 1952.

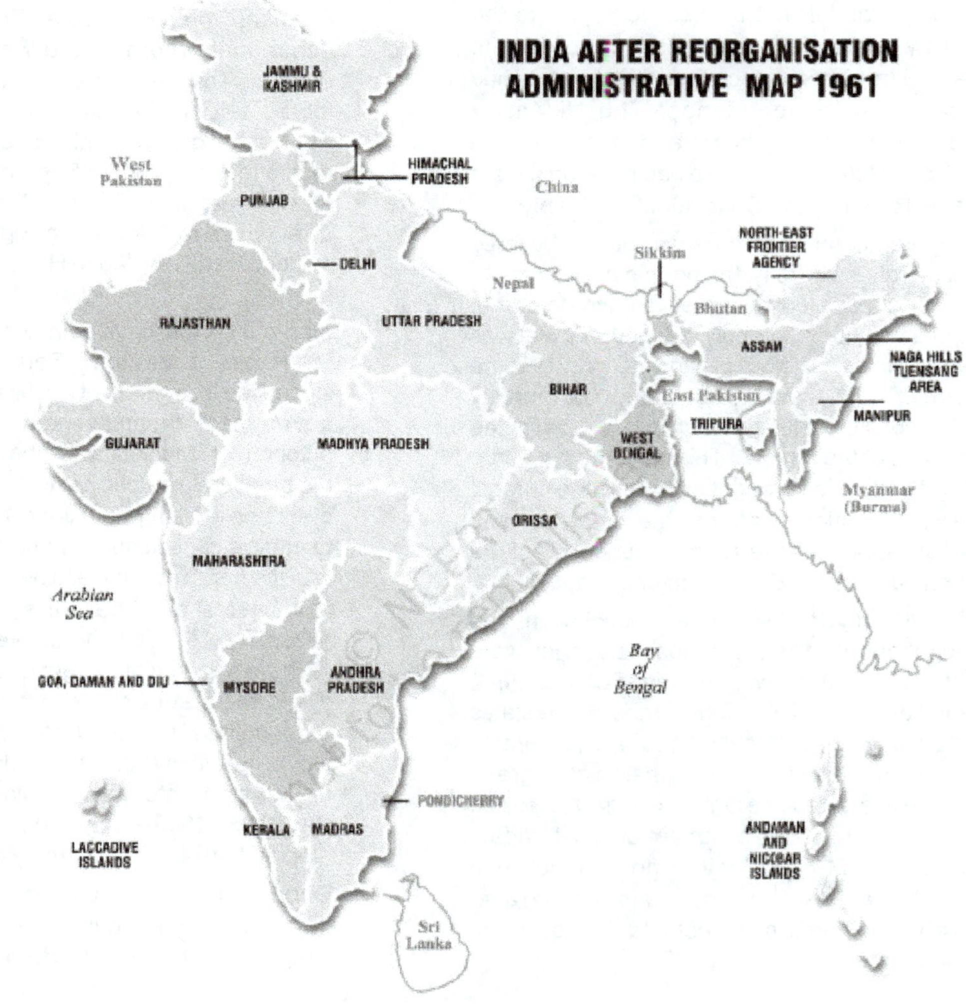

❖ The formation of Andhra spurred the struggle for making of other states on linguistic lines in other parts of the country. These struggles forced the Central Government into appointing a States Reorganisation Commission in 1953 to look into the question of redrawing of the boundaries of states. The Commission in its report accepted that the boundaries of the state should reflect the boundaries of different languages. On the basis of its report the States Reorganisation Act was passed in 1956. This led to the creation of 14 states and six union territories.

❖ Above all, the linguistic states underlined the acceptance of the principle of diversity. When we say that India adopted democracy, it does not simply mean that India embraced a democratic constitution, nor does it merely mean that India adopted the format of elections. The choice was larger than that. It was a choice in favour of recognizing and accepting the existence of differences which could at times be oppositional. Democracy, in other words, was associated with plurality of ideas and ways of life.

❖ The states of Maharashtra and Gujarat were created in 1960.

❖ Statehood for Punjab came ten years later, in 1966, when the territories of today's Haryana and Himachal Pradesh were separated from the larger Punjab state.

❖ Meghalaya was carved out of Assam in 1972. Manipur and Tripura too emerged as separate states in the same year. The states of Mizoram and Arunachal Pradesh came into being in 1987. Nagaland had become a state much earlier in 1963.

❖ Three states Chhattisgarh, Uttarakhand and Jharkhand, were created in 2000.

Exercise

Level – 1

1. The famous speech 'tryst with destiny' is given by which personality?
   (a) Rajendra Prasad
   (b) Jawaharlal Nehru
   (c) Mahatma Gandhi
   (d) Subhash Chandra Bose

2. Which of the following are the goals to be achieved after independence?
   (a) Our country is to be run through democratic government.
   (b) The government will be run for the good of all, particularly the poor and the socially disadvantaged groups.
   (c) Both (a) and (b)
   (d) Neither (a) nor (b)

3. What were the primary challenges of the independent India?
   (a) The immediate challenge was to shape a nation that was united, yet accommodative of the diversity in our society.
   (b) The second challenge was to establish democracy.
   (c) The third challenge was to ensure the development and wellbeing of the entire society and not only of some sections.
   (d) All of the above

4. In Indian constitution, which of the following is added for welfare purpose of society?
   (a) Directive Principles of State Policy
   (b) Fundamental Rights
   (c) The Principle of Equality
   (d) Democratic Principles

5. Two-nation theory is given by which of the following political party?
   (a) Congress
   (b) Muslim League
   (c) Bhartiya Janta Party
   (d) Janta Party

6. Which of the following leader is known as 'Frontier Gandhi'?
   (a) Mahatma Gandhi
   (b) Rajendra Prasad
   (c) Khan Abdul Gaffar Khan
   (d) Mohammad Ali Jinnah

7. What is the full form of NWFP?

   (a) North Western Frontier Province

   (b) North Western Frontier Part

   (c) North Ward Frontier Province

   (d) North Western Front Part

8. Which of the province has to be divided after partition?

   (a) Punjab   (b) Bengal

   (c) Both (a) and (b)   (d) Neither (a) nor (b)

9. Which of the following cities were divided into 'communal zones'?

   (a) Lahore   (b) Amritsar

   (c) Kolkata   (d) All of the above

10. What was the percentage of Muslim population in 1959 in India?

   (a) 10   (b) 12

   (c) 14   (d) 16

11. What was the total number of princely states in India at the time of independence?

   (a) 565   (b) 540

   (c) 555   (d) 560

12. Which was the first princely state that announced to be independent?

   (a) Travancore   (b) Hyderabad

   (c) Bhopal   (d) Mysore

13. What do you mean by 'Instrument of Accession'?

   (a) State agreed to become a part of the Pakistan.

   (b) State agreed to become a part of the Union of India.

   (c) State agreed to be independent.

   (d) State agreed to become a part of the British India.

14. Which of the following princely state joins India after a plebiscite?

   (a) Manipur   (b) Kashmir

   (c) Hyderabad   (d) Junagarh

15. The title of 'Nizam' belongs to which state's ruler?

   (a) Bengal   (b) Bombay

   (c) Hyderabad   (d) Madras

Level – 2

16. Razakars were the para-military force of which of the following state?

   (a) Bengal   (b) Madras

   (c) Bombay   (d) Hyderabad

17. Which of the following state was the first part of India to hold an election based on universal adult franchise?

   (a) Manipur   (b) Hyderabad

   (c) Bombay   (d) Kolkata

18. What was the basis to draw state boundaries during colonial rule?

   (a) The state boundaries were drawn on administrative convenience.

   (b) Simply coincided with the territories annexed by the British government.

   (c) Territories ruled by the princely powers.

   (d) All of the above.

19. The Vishalandhra movement is organized for which of the state?

   (a) Andhra   (b) Karnataka

   (c) Kerala   (d) Madras

20. Which of the following was the first state to be formed on the basis of language?

   (a) Madras   (b) Andhra Pradesh

   (c) Tamil Nadu   (d) Kerala

21. Potti Sriramulu went on an indefinite fast for the formation of which of the following state?

   (a) Kerala   (b) Kolkata

   (c) Andhra Pradesh   (d) Karnataka

22. In which of the following year State Reorganisation Commission was set up?

   (a) 1952   (b) 1953

   (c) 1954   (d) 1955

23. How many numbers of states and union territories were formed on the basis of the report given by State Reorganisation Commission?

   (a) 14 and 5   (b) 15 and 6

   (c) 16 and 5   (d) 14 and 6

24. Democracy word means –

   (a) It simply means that India embraced a democratic constitution.

   (b) It merely means that India adopted the format of elections.

   (c) It was associated with plurality of ideas and ways of life.

   (d) It was associated with plurality of political ideas.

25. Meghalaya was carved out from which of the following state?

   (a) Assam   (b) Manipur

   (c) Tripura   (d) Mizoram

Answer Keys

Level – 1

1. (b)	2. (c)	3. (d)	4. (a)	5. (b)	6. (c)	7. (a)	8. (c)	9. (d)	10. (b)
11. (a)	12. (a)	13. (b)	14. (d)	15. (c)					

Level – 2

16. (d)	17. (a)	18. (d)	19. (a)	20. (b)	21. (c)	22. (b)	23. (d)	24. (c)	25. (a)

Solutions

Level – 1

1. b • At the hour of midnight on 14-15 August 1947, India attained independence. Jawaharlal Nehru, the first prime minister of free India, addressed a special session of the Constituent Assembly that night. This was the famous 'tryst with destiny' speech.

2. c • There were two goals almost everyone agreed upon: one, that after independence, we shall run our country through democratic government; and two, that the government will be run for the good of all, particularly the poor and the socially disadvantaged groups.

3. d • The first and the immediate challenge were to shape a nation that was united, yet accommodative of the diversity in our society. India was a land of continental size and diversity. Its people spoke different languages and followed different cultures and religions.

• The second challenge was to establish democracy. The Constitution granted fundamental rights and extended the right to vote to every citizen. India adopted representative democracy based on the parliamentary form of government.

• The third challenge was to ensure the development and wellbeing of the entire society and not only of some sections. Here again the Constitution clearly laid down the principle of equality and special protection to socially disadvantaged groups and religious and cultural communities.

4. a • The Constitution set out in the Directive Principles of State Policy the welfare goals that democratic politics must achieve.

5. b • On 14-15 August 1947, not one but two nation-states came into existence. India and Pakistan. This was a result of 'partition', the division of British India into India and Pakistan. According to the 'two-nation theory' advanced by the Muslim League, India consisted of not one but two 'people', Hindus and Muslims. That is why it demanded Pakistan, a separate country for the Muslims. The Congress opposed this theory and the demand for Pakistan.

6. c • Not all Muslim majority areas wanted to be in Pakistan. Khan Abdul Gaffar Khan, the undisputed leader of the North Western Frontier Province and known as 'Frontier Gandhi', was staunchly opposed to the two-nation theory.

7. a • North Western Frontier Province (NWFP) was made to merge with Pakistan.

8. c • Two of the Muslim majority provinces of British India, Punjab and Bengal, had very large areas where the non-Muslims were in majority. Eventually it was decided that these two provinces would be bifurcated according to the religious majority at the district or even lower level.

9. d • Cities like Lahore, Amritsar and Kolkata became divided into 'communal zones'.

10. b • The Muslim population in India accounted for 12 per cent of the total population in 1951.

11. a • There were 565 princely states in India at the time of independence.

12. a • Just before Independence it was announced by the British that with the end of their rule over India, paramountcy of the British crown over Princely States would also lapse. This meant that all these states, as many as 565 in all, would become legally independent. The British government took the view that all these states were free to join either India or Pakistan or remain independent if they so wished. This decision was left not to the people but to the princely rulers of these states. First of all, the ruler of Travancore announced that the state had decided on Independence. The Nizam of Hyderabad made a similar announcement the next day. Rulers like the Nawab of Bhopal were averse to joining the Constituent Assembly.

13. b • Before 15 August 1947, peaceful negotiations had brought almost all states whose territories were contiguous to the new boundaries of India, into the Indian Union. The rulers of most of the states signed a document called the 'Instrument of Accession' which meant that their state agreed to become a part of the Union of India.

14. d • The issue of Junagarh was resolved after a plebiscite confirmed people's desire to join India.

15. c • Hyderabad, the largest of the Princely States was surrounded entirely by Indian Territory. Some parts of the old Hyderabad state are today parts of Maharashtra, Karnataka and Andhra Pradesh. Its ruler carried the title, 'Nizam', and he was one of the world's richest men.

Level – 2

16. d • A movement of the people of Hyderabad State against the Nizam's rule gathered force. The peasantry in the Telangana region in particular, was the victim of Nizam's oppressive rule and rose against him. Women who had seen the worst of this oppression joined the movement in large numbers. Hyderabad town was the nerve centre of this movement. The Communists and the Hyderabad Congress were in the forefront of the movement. The Nizam responded by unleashing a para-military force known as the Razakars on the people. The atrocities and communal nature of the Razakars knew no bounds. They murdered, maimed, raped and looted, targeting particularly the non-Muslims.

17. a • A few days before Independence, the Maharaja of Manipur, Bodhachandra Singh, signed the Instrument of Accession with the Indian government on the assurance that the internal autonomy of Manipur would be maintained. Under the pressure of public opinion, the Maharaja held elections in Manipur in June 1948 and the state became a constitutional monarchy. Thus Manipur was the first part of India to hold an election based on universal adult franchise.

18. d • During colonial rule, the state boundaries were drawn either on administrative convenience or simply coincided with the territories annexed by the British government or the territories ruled by the princely powers.

19. a • The Vishalandhra movement (as the movement for a separate Andhra was called) demanded that the Telugu speaking areas should be separated from the Madras province of which they were a part and be made into a separate Andhra province.

20. b • Protests began in the Telugu speaking areas of the old Madras province, which included present day Tamil Nadu, parts of Andhra Pradesh, Kerala and Karnataka. The Vishalandhra movement (as the movement for a separate Andhra was called) demanded that the Telugu speaking areas should be separated from the Madras province of which they were a part and be made into a separate Andhra province. Nearly all the political forces in the Andhra region were in favour of linguistic reorganisation of the then Madras province.

21. c • Potti Sriramulu, a Congress leader and a veteran Gandhian, went on an indefinite fast that led to his death after 56 days. This caused great unrest and resulted in violent outbursts in Andhra region. People in large numbers took to the streets. Many were injured or lost their lives in police firing. In Madras, several legislators resigned their seats in protest. Finally, the Prime Minister announced the formation of a separate Andhra state in December 1952.

22. b • The Central Government into appointing a States Reorganisation Commission in 1953 to look into the question of redrawing of the boundaries of states.

23. d • The State Reorganisation Commission in its report accepted that the boundaries of the state should reflect the boundaries of different languages. On the basis of its report the States Reorganisation Act was passed in 1956. This led to the creation of 14 states and six union territories.

24. c • Above all, the linguistic states underlined the acceptance of the principle of diversity. When we say that India adopted democracy, it does not simply mean that India embraced a democratic constitution, nor does it merely mean that India adopted the format of elections. The choice was larger than that. It was a choice in favour of recognizing and accepting the existence of differences which could at times be oppositional. Democracy, in other words, was associated with plurality of ideas and ways of life.

25. a • Another major reorganisation of states took place in the north-east in 1972. Meghalaya was carved out of Assam in 1972. Manipur and Tripura too emerged as separate states in the same year. The states of Mizoram and Arunachal Pradesh came into being in 1987. Nagaland had become a state much earlier in 1963.

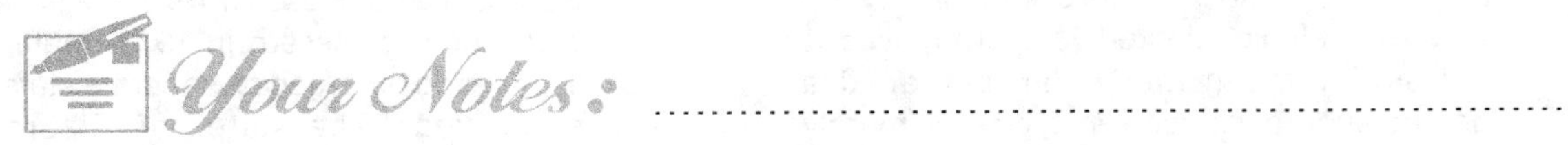
Your Notes :

Era of One-Party Dominance

Challenge of Building Democracy

The conditions in India were not very different. But the leaders of the newly independent India decided to take the more difficult path. . The Election Commission of India was set up in January 1950. Sukumar Sen became the first Chief Election Commissioner. The country's first general elections were expected sometime in 1950 itself.

But the Election Commission discovered that it was not going to be easy to hold a free and fair election in a country of India's size.

CONGRESS DOMINANCE IN THE FIRST THREE GENERAL ELECTIONS

The Congress party, as it was popularly known, had inherited the legacy of the national movement. It was the only party then to have an organization spread all over the country. And finally, in Jawaharlal Nehru, the party had the most popular and charismatic leader in Indian politics.

The party won 364 of the 489 seats in the first Lok Sabha and finished way ahead of any other challenger. The Communist Party of India that came next in terms of seats won only 16 seats.

Socialist Party:

The origins of the Socialist Party can be traced back to the mass movement stage of the Indian National Congress in the pre-independence era. In 1948, the Congress amended its constitution to prevent its members from having a dual party membership.

The socialists believed in the ideology of democratic socialism which distinguished them both from the Congress as well as from the Communists.

Nature of Congress Dominance:

India is not the only country to have experienced the dominance of one party. In some countries like China, Cuba and Syria the constitution permits only a single party to rule the country. The roots of this extraordinary success of the Congress party go back to the legacy of the freedom struggle.

Congress as social and ideological coalition:

The Congress began as a party dominated by the English speaking, upper caste, upper middle-class and urban elite. By the time of Independence, the Congress was transformed into a rainbow-like social coalition broadly representing India's diversity in terms of classes and castes, religions and languages and various interests.

The Congress was a 'platform' for numerous groups, interests and even political parties to take part in the national movement.

Tolerance and management of factions:

Coalition-like character of the Congress gave it an unusual strength. Firstly, a coalition accommodates all those who join it.

Secondly, in a party that has the nature of a coalition, there is a greater tolerance of internal differences and ambitions of various groups and leaders are accommodated.

The Congress did both these things during the freedom struggle and continued doing this even after Independence.

These groups inside the party are called factions. The coalitional nature of the Congress party tolerated and in fact encouraged various factions. Most of the state units of the Congress were made up of numerous factions. The factions took different ideological positions making the Congress appear as a grand centrist party.

They were not alternatives to the ruling party; instead they constantly pressurised and criticised, censured and influenced the Congress.

Emergence of opposition parties

Opposition_parties _presence played a crucial role in maintaining the democratic character of the system.

These parties offered a sustained and often principled criticism of the policies and practices of the Congress party.

Jawaharlal Nehru often referred to his fondness for the Socialist Party and invited socialist leaders like Jayaprakash Narayan to join his government. This kind of personal relationship with and respect for political adversaries declined after the party competition grew more intense.

Congress to accommodate all interests and all aspirants for political power steadily declined, other political parties started gaining greater significance.

Exercise

1. When Constitution of India adopted?
   - (a) 26th November,1950
   - (b) 24 January 1950
   - (c) 26 November 1949
   - (d) 26th January 1950

2. Who was the first Chief Election Commissioner of Independent India?
   - (a) Sukumar Sen
   - (b) Vinay Pathak
   - (c) BR Ambedkar
   - (d) C P Joshi

3. Who was Education Minister in the first cabinet of free India?
   - (a) Maulana Abul Kalam Azad
   - (b) Rajkumari Amrit Kaur
   - (c) Acharya Narendra Dev
   - (d) Sukumar Sen

4. Who was the founding President of the Congress Socialist Party?
   - (a) Rajkumari Amrit Kaur
   - (b) Sukumar Sen
   - (c) Acharya Narendra Dev
   - (d) Maulana Abul Kalam Azad

5. Which of the following party of India represented the legacy of the Mexican revolution?
   - (a) Indian National Congress
   - (b) Institutional Revolutionary Party
   - (c) Communist Party of India
   - (d) Congress Socialist Party

6. Who among the following leader of India adopted Buddhisim?
   - (a) Sukumar Sen
   - (b) Acharya Narendra Dev
   - (c) Maulana Abul Kalam Azad
   - (d) BR Ambedkar

7. Who was the founder of Bharatiya Jana Sangh?
   - (a) Shyama Prasad Mukherjee
   - (b) B R Ambedkar
   - (c) Dr. Shreeram Lagoo
   - (d) Mohan Agashe

8. Which of the following were not the resolutions of Swatantra Party?
   1. adoption of cooperative farming
   2. Land ceiling
   3. Heavy Industries
   4. Promotion of FDI
   Select the correct answer using the codes given below:
   - (a) 1, 2 and 3 only
   - (b) 3 and 4 only
   - (c) 2 and 3 only
   - (d) 1, 2, 3 and 4

9. Which of the following is not true about C. Rajagopalachari?
   1. first Indian to be the Governor General of India
   2. first recipient of the Bharat Ratna Award
   3. founder of the Swatantra Party
   Select the correct answer using the codes given below:
   - (a) 1 and 2 only
   - (b) 3 only
   - (c) 1, 2 and 3
   - (d) All correct

10. Who was the founder of Bharatiya Jana Sangh?
    - (a) Shyama Prasad Mukherjee
    - (b) Fanishwarnath Renu
    - (c) B R Ambedkar
    - (d) C Rajagopalchari

Answer Keys

1. (c) 2. (a) 3. (a) 4. (c) 5. (b) 6. (d) 7. (a) 8. (b) 9. (d) 10. (a)

Politics of Planned Development

As the global demand for steel increases, Orissa, which has one of the largest reserves of untapped iron ore in the country, is being seen as an important investment destination.

The iron ore resources lie in some of the most underdeveloped and predominantly tribal districts of the state. The tribal population fears that the setting up of industries would mean displacement from their home and livelihood.

Political Contestation

It is important to take advice from experts on mining, from environmentalists and from economists. Yet the final decision must be a political decision, taken by people's representatives who are in touch with the feelings of the people.

All these decisions were bound together by a shared vision or model of economic development. It was also agreed that this matter cannot be left to businessmen, industrialists and farmers themselves, that the government should play a key role in this.

Ideas of Development

Development would mean different things for example, to an industrialist who is planning to set up a steel plant, to an urban consumer of steel and to the Adivasi who lives in that region.

On the eve of Independence, India had before it, two models of modern development: the liberal-capitalist model as in much of Europe and the US and the socialist model as in the USSR.

This reflected a broad consensus that had developed during the national movement. The nationalist leaders were clear that the economic concerns of the government of free India would have to be different from the narrowly defined commercial functions of the colonial government.

Planning:

In fact the idea of planning as a process of rebuilding economy earned a good deal of public support in the 1940s and 1950s all over the world.

The Bombay Plan wanted the state to take major initiatives in industrial and other economic investments. Thus, from left to right, planning for development was the most obvious choice for the country after Independence.

The Early Initiative:

As in the USSR, the Planning Commission of India opted for five year plans (FYP). The idea is very simple: the Government of India prepares a document that has a plan for all its income and expenditure for the next five years.

The First Five Year Plan:

The First Five Year Plan (1951–1956) sought to get the country's economy out of the cycle of poverty. K.N. Raj, a young economist involved in drafting the plan, argued that India should 'hasten slowly' for the first two decades as a fast rate of development might endanger democracy. Agricultural sector was hit hardest by Partition and needed urgent attention. Huge allocations were made for large-scale projects like the Bhakhra Nangal Dam.

Rapid Industrialisation:

The Second FYP stressed on heavy industries. It was drafted by a team of economists and planners under the leadership of P. C. Mahalanobis. As savings and investment were growing in this period, a bulk of these industries like electricity, railways, steel, machineries and communication could be developed in the public sector. Indeed, such a push for industrialisation marked a turning point in India's development.

Agriculture versus industry:

Many thought that the Second Plan lacked an agrarian strategy for development, and the emphasis on industry caused agriculture and rural India to suffer. Others thought that without a drastic increase in industrial production, there could be no escape from the cycle of poverty. They argued that Indian planning did have an agrarian strategy to boost the production of foodgrains.

Public versus private sector:

India did not follow any of the two known paths to

development – it did not accept the capitalist model of development in which development was left entirely to the private sector, nor did it follow the socialist model in which private property was abolished and all the production was controlled by the state. A mixed model like this was open to criticism from both the left and the right. Critics argued that the planners refused to provide the private sector with enough space and the stimulus to grow.

The state intervened only in those areas where the private sector was not prepared to go. Thus the state helped the private sector to make profit.

Major Outcomes

Land reforms did not take place effectively in most parts of the country; political power remained in the hands of the landowning classes; and big industrialists continued to benefit and thrive while poverty did not reduce much.

Land reforms:

Perhaps the most significant and successful of these was the abolition of the colonial system of zamindari. Attempts at consolidation of land – bringing small pieces of land together in one place so that the farm size could become viable for agriculture – were also fairly successful.

It was not easy to turn these well-meaning policies on agriculture into genuine and effective action. This could happen only if the rural, landless poor were mobilised.

The Green Revolution:

The government adopted a new strategy for agriculture in order to ensure food sufficiency. Thus the government offered high-yielding variety seeds, fertilizers, pesticides and better irrigation at highly subsidised prices. The government also gave a guarantee to buy the produce of the farmers at a given price. The green revolution delivered only a moderate agricultural growth (mainly a rise in wheat production) and raised the availability of food in the country, but increased polarisation between classes and regions. Some regions like Punjab, Haryana and western Uttar Pradesh became agriculturally prosperous, while others remained backward.

Exercise

1. The Government of India replaced the Planning Commission with a new institution named NITI Aayog on ________________.
   (a) 1st January 2015
   (b) 10th February 2015
   (c) 31st March 2015
   (d) 1st April 2015

2. The Bombay Plan was drafted by ______________ of India in 1944.
   (a) Big Industrialists   (b) Big Landlords
   (c) Big Farmers   (d) Big Bankers

3. Who was drafted the First five years plan of India?
   (a) J L Nehru   (b) Sukumar sen
   (c) C Rajagopalchari (d) K.N. Raj

4. Which of the following area was the main focus behind the second five year plan?
   (a) Agricure   (b) Food export
   (c) Poverty   (d) Industrialisation.

5. Who was the founder of Indian Statistical Institute?
   (a) J.C. Kumarappa   (b) Shrilal Shukla
   (c) P.C. Mahalanobis (d) K.N Raj

6. 'Socialist pattern of society' was goal of which five year plan of India?
   (a) First Five year Plan
   (b) Second Five year plan
   (c) Third Five year Plan
   (d) Annual Plan

7. Who was the author of 'Economy of Permanence'?
   (a) P.C. Mahalanobis (b) K.N Raj
   (c) J.C. Kumarappa   (d) Shrilal Shukla

8. Who was also known as 'Milkman of India'?
   (a) Verghese Kurien   (b) Srikanth
   (c) M Swaminathan   (d) P.C. Mahalanobis

9. Who was the chairperson of planning commission?
   (a) Prime Minister
   (b) Finance Minister
   (c) Defence Minister
   (d) Chief Secretary

10. What was the reason for Plan holiday in 1966?
    (a) Acute economic crisis
    (b) BOP crisis
    (c) Inflation
    (d) World war

Answer Keys

1. (a)   2. (a)   3. (d)   4. (d)   5. (c)   6. (b)   7. (c)   8. (a)   9. (a)   10. (a)

CHAPTER 4

India's External Relations

International context:

As a nation born in the backdrop of the world war, India decided to conduct its foreign relations with an aim to respect the sovereignty of all other nations and to achieve security through the maintenance of peace. This aim finds an echo in the Directive Principles of State Policy.

In the period immediately after the Second World War, many developing nations chose to support the foreign policy preferences of the powerful countries who were giving them aid or credits.

The Policy of non-alignment:

The foreign policy of a nation reflects the interplay of domestic and external factors. Therefore, the noble ideals that inspired India's struggle for freedom influenced the making of its foreign policy.

Nehru's role

The first Prime Minister, Jawaharlal Nehru played a crucial role in setting the national agenda. He was his own foreign minister. Thus both as the Prime Minister and the Foreign Minister, he exercised profound influence in the formulation and implementation of India's foreign policy from 1946 to 1964.

The three major objectives of Nehru's foreign policy were to preserve the hard-earned sovereignty, protect territorial integrity, and promote rapid economic development.

Distance from two camps

The foreign policy of independent India vigorously pursued the dream of a peaceful world by advocating the policy of non-alignment, by reducing Cold War tensions and by contributing human resources to the UN peacekeeping operations.

India wanted to keep away from the military alliances led by US and Soviet Union against each other. While India was trying to convince the other developing countries about the policy of non-alignment, Pakistan joined the US-led military alliances.

Afro-Asian unity

Throughout the 1940s and 1950s, Nehru had been an ardent advocate of Asian unity. Under his leadership, India convened the Asian Relations Conference in March 1947, five months ahead of attaining its independence. The AfroAsian conference held in the Indonesian city of Bandung in 1955, commonly known as the Bandung Conference, marked the zenith of India's engagement with the newly independent Asian and African nations. The Bandung Conference later led to the establishment of the NAM. The First Summit of the NAM was held in Belgrade in September 1961. Nehru was a co-founder of the NAM.

Peace and conflict with China :

Unlike its relationship with Pakistan, free India began its relationship with China on a very friendly note. After the Chinese revolution in 1949, India was one of the first countries to recognise the communist government.

The Chinese invasion, 1962:

The Tibetan spiritual leader, the Dalai Lama, sought and obtained political asylum in India in 1959. China alleged that the government of India was allowing anti-China activities to take place from within India.

China claimed two areas within the Indian territory: Aksai-chin area in the Ladakh region of Jammu and Kashmir and much of the state of Arunachal Pradesh in what was then called NEFA (North Eastern Frontier Agency). China launched a swift and massive invasion in October 1962 on both the disputed regions.

The China war dented India's image at home and abroad. India had to approach the Americans and the British for military assistance to tide over the crisis. The Soviet Union remained neutral during the conflict. It induced a sense of national humiliation and at the same time strengthened a spirit of nationalism. The party split in 1964 and the leaders of the latter faction formed the Communist Party of India (Marxist) (CPI-M).

The process of its reorganization began soon after the China war. Nagaland was granted statehood; Manipur and

Tripura, though Union Territories were given the right to elect their own legislative assemblies.

Wars and Peace with Pakistan

The Kashmir conflict did not prevent cooperation between the governments of India and Pakistan. Both the governments worked together to restore the women abducted during Partition to their original families. The IndiaPakistan Indus Waters Treaty was signed by Nehru and General Ayub Khan in 1960.

A more serious armed conflict between the two countries began in 1965. As you would read in the next chapter, by then Lal Bahadur Shastri had taken over as the Prime Minister. In April 1965 Pakistan launched armed attacks in the Rann of Kutch area of Gujarat.

The hostilities came to an end with the UN intervention. Later, Indian Prime Minister Lal Bahadur Shastri and Pakistan's General Ayub Khan signed the Tashkent Agreement, brokered by the Soviet Union, in January 1966.

Bangladesh war, 1971

Beginning in 1970, Pakistan faced its biggest internal crisis. The country's first general election produced a split verdict – Zulfikar Ali Bhutto's party emerged a winner in West Pakistan, while the Awami League led by Sheikh Mujib-ur Rahman swept through East Pakistan.

Instead, in early 1971, the Pakistani army arrested Sheikh Mujib and unleashed a reign of terror on the people of East Pakistan.

In response to this, the people started a struggle to liberate 'Bangladesh' from Pakistan. Throughout 1971, India had to bear the burden of about 80 lakh refugees who fled East Pakistan and took shelter in the neighbouring areas in India. India extended moral and material support to the freedom struggle in Bangladesh. Pakistan accused India of a conspiracy to break it up.

Support for Pakistan came from the US and China. In order to counter the US-Pakistan-China axis, India signed a 20-year Treaty of Peace and Friendship with the Soviet Union in August 1971. This treaty assured India of Soviet support if the country faced any attack.

After months of diplomatic tension and military build-up, a full-scale war between India and Pakistan broke out in December 1971. Welcomed and supported by the local population, the Indian army made rapid progress in East Pakistan. Within ten days the Indian army had surrounded Dhaka from three sides and the Pakistani army of about 90,000 had to surrender. With Bangladesh as a free country, India declared a unilateral ceasefire. Later, the signing of the Shimla Agreement between Indira Gandhi and Zulfikar Ali Bhutto on 3 July 1972 formalized the return of peace.

India, with its limited resources, had initiated development planning. However, conflicts with neighbours derailed the five-year plans. The scarce resources were diverted to the defence sector especially after 1962, as India had to embark on a military modernisation drive.

India's nuclear policy

Another crucial development of this period was the first nuclear explosion undertaken by India in May 1974. Nehru had always put his faith in science and technology for rapidly building a modern India. A significant component of his industrialisation plans was the nuclear programme initiated in the late 1940s under the guidance of Homi J. Bhabha.

When Communist China conducted nuclear tests in October 1964, the five nuclear weapon powers, the US, USSR, UK, France, and China (Taiwan then represented China) – also the five Permanent Members of the UN Security Council – tried to impose the Nuclear Non-proliferation Treaty (NPT) of 1968 on the rest of the world. India always considered the NPT as discriminatory and had refused to sign it.

When India conducted its first nuclear test, it was termed as peaceful explosion. India argued that it was committed to the policy of using nuclear power only for peaceful purposes.

The period when the nuclear test was conducted was a difficult period in domestic politics. Following the Arab-Israel War of 1973, the entire world was affected by the Oil Shock due to the massive hike in the oil prices by the Arab nations. It led to economic turmoil in India resulting in high inflation.

Exercise

1. Which of the following were not the objectives of Nehru's foreign policy?
   (a) to preserve the hard-earned sovereignty
   (b) protect territorial integrity
   (c) promote rapid economic development
   (d) to participate in cold war in support of USSR.

2. What was the region where British attacked Egypt in 1956?
   (a) Panama Canal
   (b) Suez Canal
   (c) Mediterranean canal
   (d) Caspian canal

3. Under which of the following country leadership Asian Relations Conference convened in March 1947?
   (a) India
   (b) China
   (c) South Africa
   (d) Egypt

4. Bandung Conference was held in the year:
   (a) 1954
   (b) 1955
   (c) 1956
   (d) 1957

5. Bangladesh emerged as an independent nation in:
   (a) January 1972
   (b) December 1971
   (c) March 1971
   (d) November 1971

6. The First Summit of the NAM was held in __________.
   (a) Belgrade
   (b) Sydney
   (c) Bandung
   (d) Kathmandu

7. The joint enunciation of Panchsheel was set up between India and ______.
   (a) Nepal
   (b) Pakistan
   (c) China
   (d) Bangladesh

8. Which of the following area were claimed by china?
   (a) Aksai Chin
   (b) Sir Creek
   (c) Punjab
   (d) Manipur

9. The Architect of Non-alignment is:
   (a) Pt. Nehru
   (b) Indira Gandhi
   (c) Y. B. Chavan
   (d) Atal Behari Vajpayee

10. What was the reason of China attack on India in October 1962?
    (a) India given political asylum to Dalai Lama.
    (b) India supported Bangladesh Liberation of war.
    (c) India tested Nuclear Missile
    (d) India supported NAM

11. Bangladesh emerged as an independent nation in:
    (a) January 1972
    (b) December 1971
    (c) March 1971
    (d) November 1971

12. Treaty of Peace and Friendship in August 1971 was signed between which two countries?
    (a) India and US
    (b) India and Bangladesh
    (c) India and Soviet Union
    (d) India and China

13. Tashkent Agreement was brokered by __________.
    (a) World Bank
    (b) US
    (c) Soviet Union
    (d) United Nation

14. In which year India Pakistan Indus water treaty was signed?
    (a) 1960
    (b) 1965
    (c) 1962
    (d) 1959

15. Shimla agreement was signed on __________.
    (a) 3 July 1972
    (b) 4 July 1972
    (c) 11 July 1972
    (d) 3 July 1971

16. The Department of Defence Production was established __________.
    (a) November 1963
    (b) December 1962
    (c) November 1962
    (d) November 1961

17. Nuclear programme in India was initiated under the guidance of __________.
    (a) JL Nehru
    (b) CV Raman
    (c) Homi J. Bhabha
    (d) Jagdish Mohan

18. In which year Nuclear Non-proliferation Treaty (NPT) was imposed?
    (a) 1968
    (b) 1969
    (c) 1970
    (d) 1971

19. Which of the following was the reason behind for Oil Shock in 1973?
    (a) Arab-Israel War
    (b) US attack on USSR
    (c) Discovery of Oil in US
    (d) China decreases oil price

20. After the Chinese revolution in 1949, which country was the first to recognize the Communist Government?
    (a) Bangladesh
    (b) Pakistan
    (c) India
    (d) USSR

21. "no first use" doctrine of Indian policy is associated with which of the following?

    (a) Nuclear Doctrine   (b) Look east policy

    (c) Border violation   (d) UN charter

22. Which of the following place in India is the largest refuge settlement of Tibetans in India?

    (a) Leh

    (b) Sikkim

    (c) Imphal

    (d) Dharmshala in Himachal Pradesh

23. Which of the following was the reason behind for not started 3rd Five year Plan?

    (a) Import of Rice was banned by US

    (b) Infrastructure expenditure was high

    (c) Conflicts with neighbours countries

    (d) Death of Prime Minister

Answer Keys

1. (d)	2. (b)	3. (a)	4. (b)	5. (b)	6. (a)	7. (c)	8. (a)	9. (a)	10. (a)
11. (b)	12. (c)	13. (c)	14. (a)	15. (a)	16. (c)	17. (c)	18. (a)	19. (a)	20. (c)
21. (a)	22. (d)	23. (c)							

CHAPTER 5

Challenges to and Restoration of The Congress System

Challenge of Political Succession

Prime Minister Jawaharlal Nehru passed away in May 1964. The 1960s were labelled as the 'dangerous decade' when unresolved problems like poverty, inequality, communal and regional divisions etc. could lead to a failure of the democratic project or even the disintegration of the country.

From Nehru to Shastri:

Shastri was the country's Prime Minister from 1964 to 1966. During Shastri's brief Prime Ministership, the country faced two major challenges. While India was still recovering from the economic implications of the war with China, failed monsoons, drought and serious food crisis presented a grave challenge. The country also faced a war with Pakistan in 1965. Shastri's famous slogan 'Jai Jawan Jai Kisan', symbolised the country's resolve to face both these challenges.

Shastri's Prime Ministership came to an abrupt end on 10 January 1966, when he suddenly expired in Tashkent, then in USSR and currently the capital of Uzbekistan.

From Shastri to Indira Gandhi

Within a year of becoming Prime Minister, Indira Gandhi had to lead the party in a Lok Sabha election. Around this time, the economic situation in the country had further deteriorated, adding to her problems.

Fourth General Elections, 1967

One of the first decisions of the Indira Gandhi government was to devaluate the Indian rupee, under what was seen to be pressure from the US. Earlier one US dollar could be purchased for less than Rs. 5; after devaluation it cost more than Rs. 7.

People started protesting against the increase in prices of essential commodities, food scarcity, growing unemployment and the overall economic condition in the country.

Non-Congressism

Opposition parties were in the forefront of organising public protests and pressurising the government. Parties opposed to the Congress realised that the division of their votes kept the Congress in power.

The socialist leader Ram Manohar Lohia gave this strategy the name of 'non-Congressism'. He also produced a theoretical argument in its defence: Congress rule was undemocratic and opposed to the interests of ordinary poor people; therefore, the coming together of the non-Congress parties was necessary for reclaiming democracy for the people.

Electoral verdict

The Congress was facing the electorate for the first time without Nehru. The Congress lost majority in as many as seven States. In Madras State (now called Tamil Nadu), a regional party — the Dravida Munnetra Kazhagam (DMK) – came to power by securing a clear majority.

Coalitions

The elections of 1967 brought into picture the phenomenon of coalitions. Since no single party had got majority, various non-Congress parties came together to form joint legislative parties (called Samyukt Vidhayak Dal in Hindi) that supported non-Congress governments. That is why these governments came to be described as SVD governments.

Defection

Defection means an elected representative leaves the party on whose symbol he/she was elected and joins another party. The constant realignments and shifting political loyalties in this period gave rise to the expression 'Aya Ram, Gaya Ram'.

Split in the Congress

We saw that after the 1967 elections, the Congress retained power at the Centre but with a reduced majority and lost power in many States.

Indira vs. the 'Syndicate'

The Syndicate had played a role in the installation of Indira Gandhi as the Prime Minister by ensuring her election as the leader of the parliamentary party. Indira Gandhi adopted a very bold strategy. She converted a simple power struggle into an ideological struggle. She launched a series of initiatives to give the government policy a Left orientation.

Presidential election, 1969

Following President Zakir Hussain's death, the post of President of the India fell vacant that year. Indira Gandhi retaliated by encouraging the then Vice-President, V.V. Giri, to file his nomination as an independent candidate. She also announced several big and popular policy measures like the nationalisation of fourteen leading private banks and the abolition of the 'privy purse' or the special privileges given to former princes. Morarji Desai was the Deputy Prime Minister and Finance Minister.

The election ultimately resulted in the victory of V.V. Giri, the independent candidate, and the defeat of Sanjeeva Reddy, the official Congress candidate.

The 1971 Election and Restoration of Congress

In order to end her dependence on other political parties, strengthen her party's position in the Parliament, and seek a popular mandate for her programmes, Indira Gandhi's government recommended the dissolution of the Lok Sabha in December 1970.

The contest

Indira Gandhi said that the opposition alliance had only one common programme: Indira Hatao (Remove Indira). In contrast to this, she put forward a positive programme captured in the famous slogan: Garibi Hatao (Remove Poverty). She focused on the growth of the public sector, imposition of ceiling on rural land holdings and urban property, removal of disparities in income and opportunity, and abolition of princely privileges.

The outcome and after

Indira Gandhi's Congress(R) won 352 seats with about 44 per cent of the popular votes on its own.

With this the Congress party led by Indira Gandhi established its claim to being the 'real' Congress and restored to it the dominant position in Indian politics. The Congress was now in power in almost all the States. It was also popular across different social sections. Within a span of four years, Indira Gandhi had warded off the challenge to her leadership and to the dominant position of the Congress party.

Restoration

Despite being more popular, the new Congress did not have the kind of capacity to absorb all tensions and conflicts that the Congress system was known for. The popular unrest and mobilisation around issues of development and economic deprivation continued to grow.

Exercise

1. Prime Minister Pt. Jawaharlal Nehru passed away in:
   - (a) January 1964
   - (b) May 1965
   - (c) March 1964
   - (d) May 1964

2. Which of the following decade described as 'Dangerous Decade'?
   - (a) 1970s
   - (b) 1960s
   - (c) 1980s
   - (d) 1950s

3. Who was the congress President at the time of Nehru death?
   - (a) Indira Gandhi
   - (b) Lal bahadur Shastri
   - (c) K.Kamraj
   - (d) Moraji Desai

4. Who was resigned from the position of Railway Minister after the major rail accident?
   - (a) Indira Gandhi
   - (b) Sardar patel
   - (c) Lal Bahadur Shastri
   - (d) Morarji Desai

5. Who was the founder of the Congress Socialist Party?
   - (a) C. Natarajan Amadurai
   - (b) Ram Manohar Lohia
   - (c) S. Nijalingappa
   - (d) K. Kamraj

6. Who was given the famous slogan 'Jai Jawan Jai Kisan'?
   - (a) S. Nijalingappa
   - (b) Indira Gandhi
   - (c) Lal Bahadur Shastri
   - (d) Moraji Desai

7. Which candidate was supported by Smt. Indira Gandhi for 1969 presidential elections?
   - (a) N. Sanjeeva Reddy
   - (b) Zakir Hussain
   - (c) V.V. Giri
   - (d) Morarji Desai

8. In which state Dravida Munnetra Kazhagam (DMK) came to power by securing a clear majority?
   - (a) Maharshtra
   - (b) Bihar
   - (c) Tamil Nadu
   - (d) Karnataka

9. Who was given the famous slogan 'Aya Ram and Gaya Ram'?
   - (a) Rao Birendra Singh
   - (b) K. Kamaraj
   - (c) Gaya Lal
   - (d) Digvijay singh

10. Who among the following was not associated with 'Syndicate'?
    - (a) K. Kamraj
    - (b) S. K. Patil
    - (c) S. Nijalingappa
    - (d) Karpoori Thakur

11. Who was introducing reservations for the backward classes in Bihar during his second Chief Ministership?
    - (a) Karpoori Thakur
    - (b) S. Nijalingappa
    - (c) S. K. Patil
    - (d) K. Kamraj

12. What was the portfolio assigned to Indira Gandhi during Lal Bahadur shastri Prime ministership?
    - (a) Foreign Minister
    - (b) Finance Minister
    - (c) Defence Minister
    - (d) Minister of Information and Broadcasting

13. Which of the following statement is sign of maturity of India's democracy?
    - (a) Coalition government
    - (b) Anti-Defection law after 1967 election
    - (c) Lok sabha and rajya sabha election
    - (d) A peaceful transition of power, despite intense competition for leadership

14. "Congress rule was undemocratic and opposed to the interests of ordinary poor people" statement was said by ______________?
    - (a) Moraji Desai
    - (b) K. Kamraj
    - (c) C. . Natarajan Annadurai
    - (d) Ram manohar Lohia

15. Which of the General election year results was considered as 'Political earthquake'?
    - (a) 1957
    - (b) 1967
    - (c) 1977
    - (d) 1972

16. Which Prime Minister of India was supported the abolition of 'privy purse'.?
    - (a) Morarji Desai
    - (b) Indiara Gandhi
    - (c) JL Nehru
    - (d) Lal bahadur shastri

17. The Indian Prime minister who gave the slogan "Garibi Hatao" was____________.
    - (a) Indira Gandhi
    - (b) Morarji desai
    - (c) V.V giri
    - (d) JL Nehru

18. When the fifth general election was was held in India?
    - (a) February 1972
    - (b) March 1971
    - (c) February 1971
    - (d) February 1973

19. Which of the following Political party was not the part of 'Grand alliance' as non-congress alliance?
   (a) Bharatiya Kranti Dal
   (b) Bharatiya Jana Sangh
   (c) Swatantra Party
   (d) CPI

20. With respect to "Ten point programme", Consider the following statements:
   (a) Social control of banks
   (b) Nationalisation of General Insurance
   (c) Ceiling on urban property and income
   (d) Heavy industries

Answer Keys

1. (d)	2. (b)	3. (c)	4. (c)	5. (b)	6. (c)	7. (c)	8. (c)	9. (c)	10. (d)
11. (a)	12. (d)	13. (d)	14. (d)	15. (b)	16. (b)	17. (a)	18. (c)	19. (d)	20. (d)

The Crisis of Democratic Order

Economic context

The Bangladesh crisis had put a heavy strain on India's economy. About eight million people crossed over the East Pakistan border into India. This was followed by war with Pakistan. After the war the U.S government stopped all aid to India. In the international market, oil prices increased manifold during this period.

Prices increased by 23 per cent in 1973 and 30 per cent in 1974. Such a high level of inflation caused much hardship to the people.

Monsoons failed in 1972-1973. This resulted in a sharp decline in agricultural productivity. Food grain output declined by 8 per cent.

There was also an increase in the activities of Marxist groups who did not believe in parliamentary politics. These groups had taken to arms and insurgent techniques for the overthrow of the capitalist order and the established political system.

GUJARAT AND BIHAR MOVEMENTS

In January 1974 students in Gujarat started an agitation against rising prices of food grains, cooking oil and other essential commodities, and against corruption in high places.

Under intense pressure from students, supported by the opposition political parties, assembly elections were held in Gujarat in June 1975.

Jayaprakash Narayan demanded the dismissal of the Congress government in Bihar and gave a call for total revolution in the social, economic and political spheres in order to establish what he considered to be true democracy.

Jayaprakash Narayan wanted to spread the Bihar movement to other parts of the country. Alongside the agitation led by Jayaprakash Narayan, the employees of the Railways gave a call for a nationwide strike.

CONFLICT WITH JUDICIARY

This was also the period when the government and the ruling party had many differences with the judiciary. Two developments further added to the tension between the judiciary and the executive. Immediately after the Supreme Court's decision in 1973 in the Keshavananda Bharati case, a vacancy arose for the post of the Chief Justice of India.

DECLARATION OF EMERGENCY:

This order came on an election petition filed by Raj Narain, a socialist leader and a candidate who had contested against her in 1971. The petition, challenged the election of Indira Gandhi on the ground that she had used the services of government servants in her election campaign.

CRISIS AND RESPONSE:

The opposition political parties led by Jayaprakash Narayan pressed for Indira Gandhi's resignation and organised a massive demonstration in Delhi's Ramlila grounds on 25 June 1975. Jayaprakash announced a nationwide satyagraha for her resignation and asked the army, the police and government employees not to obey "illegal and immoral orders".

The response of the government was to declare a state of emergency. On 25 June 1975, the government declared that there was a threat of internal disturbances and therefore, it invoked Article 352 of the Constitution.

Once an emergency is proclaimed, the federal distribution of powers remains practically suspended and all the powers are concentrated in the hands of the union government.

On the night of 25 June 1975, the Prime Minister recommended the imposition of Emergency to President Fakhruddin Ali Ahmed. He issued the proclamation immediately. After midnight, the electricity to all the major newspaper offices was disconnected.

CONSEQUENCES:

Deciding to use its special powers under Emergency provisions, the government suspended the freedom of the Press. Newspapers were asked to get prior approval for all material to be published. This is known as press censorship. Several High Courts gave judgments that even after the declaration of Emergency the courts could entertain a writ of habeas corpus filed by a person challenging his/her detention.

Many journalists were arrested for writing against the Emergency. The forty-second amendment was also passed during the Emergency. Among the various changes made by this amendment, one was that the duration of the legislatures in the country was extended from five to six years. Besides this, during an Emergency, elections can be postponed by one year.

CONTROVERSIES REGARDING EMERGENCY:

As the investigations by the Shah Commission after the Emergency found out, there were many 'excesses' committed during the Emergency.

WAS THE EMERGENCY NECESSARY?

The Constitution simply mentioned 'internal disturbances' as the reason for declaring Emergency. Some other parties, like the CPI that continued to back the Congress during the Emergency, also believed that there was an international conspiracy against the unity of India. On the other hand, the critics of the Emergency argued that ever since the freedom movement, Indian politics had a history of popular struggles. JP and many other opposition leaders felt that in a democracy, people had the right to publicly protest against the government.

WHAT HAPPENED DURING EMERGENCY?

The government said that it wanted to use the Emergency to bring law and order, restore efficiency, and above all, implement the pro-poor welfare programmes. For this purpose, the government led by Indira Gandhi announced a twentypoint programme and declared its determination to implement this programme. The twenty-point programme included land reforms, land redistribution, review of agricultural wages, workers' participation in management, eradication of bonded labour, etc.

Lessons of the Emergency

The Emergency at once brought out both the weaknesses and the strengths of India's democracy. Emergency made everyone more aware of the value of civil liberties. The Courts too, have taken an active role after the Emergency in protecting the civil liberties of the individuals. the actual implementation of the Emergency rule took place through the police and the administration. These institutions could not function independently.

POLITICS AFTER EMERGENCY

The 1977 elections turned into a referendum on the experience of the Emergency, at least in north India where the impact of the Emergency was felt most strongly. The lesson was clear and has been reiterated in many state level elections thereafter – governments that are perceived to be anti-democratic are severely punished by the voters.

Lok Sabha Elections, 1977

Accordingly, all the leaders and activists were released from jails. Elections were held in March 1977. This left the opposition with very little time, but political developments took place very rapidly.

The Janata Party made this election into a referendum on the Emergency. Its campaign was focused on the non-democratic character of the rule and on the various excesses that took place during this period.

JANATA GOVERNMENT

The Janata Party government that came to power after the 1977 elections was far from cohesive. The opposition to Emergency could keep the Janata Party together only for a while. Its critics felt that the Janata Party lacked direction, leadership, and a common programme.

The Janata Party split and the government which was led by Morarji Desai lost its majority in less than 18 months. Another government headed by Charan Singh was formed on the assurance of the support of the Congress party.

LEGACY

The Congress party now identified itself with a particular ideology, claiming to be the only socialist and pro-poor party. Thus with the early nineteen seventies, the Congress's political success depended on attracting people on the basis of sharp social and ideological divisions and the appeal of one leader, Indira Gandhi.

The issue of reservations for 'other backward classes' became very controversial in Bihar and following this, the Mandal Commission was appointed by the Janata Party government at the centre.

The Emergency and the period around it can be described as a period of constitutional crisis because it had its origins in the constitutional battle over the jurisdiction of the Parliament and the judiciary.

Exercise

1. Which of the following was not the reason of 1974 Bihar protest?
   - (a) Food scarcity
   - (b) Corruption
   - (c) Flood
   - (d) Unemployment

2. In which state Nav Nirman Movement was started?
   - (a) Bihar
   - (b) Gujrat
   - (c) Tamil Nadu
   - (d) Jammu and Kashmir

3. Who was the President of India at the time of Proclamation of emergency in 1975?
   - (a) V.V Giri
   - (b) Fakhruddin Ali Ahmed
   - (c) Neelam Sanjiva Reddy
   - (d) Giani Zail singh

4. What was the reason for declaration of National emergency in 1975?
   - (a) Threat of Internal disturbance
   - (b) No confidence motion was passed against ruling party
   - (c) Death of Prime minister
   - (d) External disturbance

5. Which of the following organization was banned during National emergency?
   1. Rashtriya Swayamsevak Sangh (RSS)
   2. Jamait-e-Islami.
   3. Socialist Party
   4. Janata Party

   Select the correct answer using the codes given below:
   - (a) 1 and 2 only
   - (b) 1, 2 and 3
   - (c) 3 and 4 only
   - (d) 1, 2, 3 and 4

6. In which year Keshavnanda Bharti case was passed by Supreme court?
   - (a) 1973
   - (b) 1975
   - (c) 1974
   - (d) 1976

7. Which article of the constitution of India is related to National emergency?
   - (a) Article 356
   - (b) Article 352
   - (c) Article 354
   - (d) Article 360

8. Which commission was appointed for the enquiry of national emergency in 1977?
   - (a) Mandal commission
   - (b) Narayan commission
   - (c) Shah commission
   - (d) Dhar commission

9. Which of the following constitutional amendment was passed during national emergency?
   - (a) 44th Constitutional amendment Act
   - (b) 42nd Constitutional amendment Act
   - (c) 45th Constitutional amendment Act
   - (d) 46th Constitutional amendment Act

10. Which of the following magazines were banned during national emergency?
    1. Seminar
    2. Frontline
    3. India today
    4. Mainstream

    Select the correct answer using the codes given below:
    - (a) 1 and 3 only
    - (b) 2 and 3 only
    - (c) 1 and 4 only
    - (d) 3 and 4 only

11. What was the reason behind for the controversial judgment of the Supreme Court?
    - (a) During Emergency the government could take away the citizen's right to life and liberty.
    - (b) Suspended the freedom of the Press
    - (c) the federal distribution of powers remains practically suspended
    - (d) Indira Gandhi will not take part in proceeding of Lok sabha

12. Who among the following election was not challenged in any court, as per amendment made by Parliament during national emergency?
    - (a) Prime Minister
    - (b) President
    - (c) Vice President
    - (d) All the above

13. What are the important lessons we get from emergency?
    1. It is extremely difficult to do away with democracy in India.
    2. Emergency made everyone more aware of the value of civil liberties.

    Which of the statements given above is/are correct?
    - (a) 1 only
    - (b) 2 only
    - (c) Both
    - (d) None

14. Who was the first Prime Minister belonging to a non-Congress party?

  (a) P V Narsimha Rao

  (b) Jayaprakash Narayan

  (c) Morarji Desai

  (d) Jagjivan Ram

15. Who was the person behind the railway strike of 1974?

  (a) Jayaprakash Narayan

  (b) Indira Gandhi

  (c) Sanjay Gandhi

  (d) George Fernandes

Answer Keys

1. (c)	2. (b)	3. (b)	4. (a)	5. (a)	6. (a)	7. (b)	8. (c)	9. (b)	10. (c)
11. (a)	12. (d)	13. (c)	14. (c)	15. (d)					

CHAPTER 7

Rise of Popular Movements

Chipko movement

- Location- Uttarakhand in early 1973
- Villagers protested against the practices of commercial logging that the government had permitted.
- They used a novel tactic for their protest – that of hugging the trees to prevent them from being cut down.
- The struggle soon spread across many parts of the Uttarakhand region.
- Larger issues of ecological and economic exploitation of the region were raised.
- The villagers demanded that no forest-exploiting contracts should be given to outsiders and local communities should have effective control over natural resources like land, water and forests.
- The movement took up economic issues of landless forest workers and asked for guarantees of minimum wage.
- Women's active participation in the Chipko agitation was a very novel aspect of the movement.
- The movement achieved a victory when the government issued a ban on felling of trees in the Himalayan regions for fifteen years
- The Chipko movement, which started over a single issue, became a symbol of many such popular movements emerging in different parts of the country during the 1970s and later.

Party based movements

- Popular movements may take the form of social movements or political movements
- Example of Political movement - nationalist movement
- Example of Social movements - the anti-caste movement, the *kisan sabhas* and the trade union movement in early twentieth century. These movements raised issues related to some underlying social conflicts.
- The peasants' and the workers' movements mainly focussed on issues of economic injustice and inequality.
- These movements did not participate in elections formally.

Non-party Movements

- In the 1970s and 1980s, many sections of the society became disillusioned with the functioning of political parties.
- In spite of the impressive growth in many sectors of economy in the first twenty years of independence, poverty and inequalities persisted on a large scale.
- A sense of injustice and deprivation grew among different groups.
- Many of the politically active groups lost faith in existing democratic institutions and electoral politics.
- They therefore chose to step outside of party politics and engage in mass mobilisation for registering their protests.
- Because of the voluntary nature of their social work, many of these organisations came to be known as voluntary organisations or voluntary sector organisations.
- These voluntary organisations chose to remain outside party politics.
- They did not contest elections at the local or regional level nor did they support any one political party.
- These organisations were called 'non-party political formations'.

- They hoped that direct participation by people will reform the nature of democratic government.

Dalit Panthers

- Dalit Panthers, a militant organisation of the Dalit youth, was formed in Maharashtra in 1972
- In the post-Independence period, Dalit groups were mainly fighting against the perpetual caste based inequalities and material injustices
- Effective implementation of reservations and other such policies of social justice was one of their prominent demands.
- The Dalit Panthers resorted to mass action for assertion of Dalits' rights.
- As a result of sustained agitations, the government passed a comprehensive law in 1989 that provided rigorous punishment for doing atrocities on Dalits
- The movement provided a platform for Dalit educated youth to use their creativity as a protest activity.
- In the post- Emergency period, Dalit Panthers got involved in electoral compromises which led to its decline.
- Organisations like the Backward and Minority Communities' Employees Federation (BAMCEF) took over this space.

Bharatiya Kisan Union

- Meerut agitation - January 1988
- Around twenty thousand farmers had gathered in the city of Meerut, Uttar Pradesh.
- They were protesting against the government decision to increase electricity rates.
- The farmers camped for about three weeks outside the district collector's office until their demands were fulfilled.
- The Meerut agitation was seen as a great show of rural power – power of farmer cultivators.
- These agitating farmers were members of the Bharatiya Kisan Union (BKU), an organisation of farmers from western Uttar Pradesh and Haryana regions.
- The BKU was one of the leading organisations in the farmers' movement of the eighties.
- Most of the BKU members belonged to a single community.
- The organisation used traditional caste panchayats of these communities in bringing them together over economic issues.

- The BKU distanced itself from all political parties. It operated as a pressure group in politics with its strength of sheer numbers.
- Like the BKU, farmers' organisations across States recruited their members from communities that dominated regional electoral politics.
- Shetkari Sanghatana of Maharashtra and Rayata Sangha of Karnataka, are prominent examples of such organisations of the farmers.

Anti-Arrack Movement

- When the BKU was mobilising the farmers of the north, an altogether different kind of mobilisation in the rural areas was taking shape in the southern State of Andhra Pradesh.
- It was a spontaneous mobilisation of women demanding a ban on the sale of alcohol in their neighbourhoods.
- Rural women in remote villages from the State of Andhra Pradesh fought a battle against alcoholism, against mafias and against the government during this period (1992).
- These agitations shaped what was known as the anti-arrack movement in the State.

Origins

- In a village in the interior of Dubagunta in Nellore district of Andhra Pradesh.
- The habit of alcoholism had taken deep roots among the village people and was ruining their physical and mental health.
- Women were the worst sufferers of these ill-effects of alcohol.
- It resulted in the collapse of the family economy and women had to bear the brunt of violence from the male family.
- Women in Nellore came together in spontaneous local initiatives to protest against arrack and forced closure of the wine shop.

Linkages

- Gradually this anti-arrack movement touched upon larger social, economic and political issues of the region that affected women's life.
- Groups of local women tried to address these complex issues in their agitation against arrack. They also openly discussed the issue of domestic violence.
- Their movement, for the first time, provided a platform to discuss private issues of domestic violence.

- Thus, the anti-arrack movement also became part of the women's movement.
- As a result the movement made demands of equal representation to women in politics during the nineties. (73rd and 74th amendments have granted reservations to women in local level political offices.)

Narmada Bachao Aandolan

- An ambitious developmental project was launched in the Narmada valley of central India in early eighties.
- The project consisted of 30 big dams, 135 medium sized and around 3,000 small dams to be constructed on the Narmada and its tributaries that flow across three states of Madhya Pradesh, Gujarat and Maharashtra.
- Sardar Sarovar Project in Gujarat and the Narmada Sagar Project in Madhya Pradesh were two of the most important and biggest, multi-purpose dams planned under the project.
- Narmada Bachao Aandolan, a movement to save Narmada , opposed the construction of these dams.

Sardar Sarovar Project

- It is a multipurpose mega-scale dam.
- In the process of construction of the dam 245 villages from these States were expected to get submerged.
- It required relocation of around two and a half lakh people from these villages.
- Issues of relocation and proper rehabilitation of the project-affected people were first raised by local activist groups.
- It was around 1988-89 that the issues crystallised under the banner of the NBA – a loose collective of local voluntary organisations.

Demands raised by the voluntary organisations

- The movement demanded proper and just rehabilitation of all those who were directly or indirectly affected by the project.
- The movement also questioned the nature of decision-making processes that go in the making of mega scale developmental projects.
- The NBA insisted that local communities must have a say in such decisions and they should also have effective control over natural resources like water, land and forests.

Achievement of the movement

- Right to rehabilitation has been now recognised by the government and the judiciary.
- A comprehensive National Rehabilitation Policy formed by the government in 2003.

Construction of the dam

- The Supreme Court upheld the government's decision to go ahead with the construction of the dam while also instructing to ensure proper rehabilitation.

The course of NBA

- Narmada Bachao Aandolan continued a sustained agitation for more than twenty years.
- It used every available democratic strategy to put forward its demands.
- However, the movement could not garner much support among the mainstream political parties – including the opposition parties.
- By the end of the 'nineties, however, the NBA was not alone.
- There emerged many local groups and movements that challenged the logic of large scale developmental projects in their areas.

Movement for Right to Information

- The movement started in 1990, when a mass based organisation called the Mazdoor Kisan Shakti Sangathan (MKSS) in Rajasthan took the initiative in demanding records of famine relief work and accounts of labourers.
- In 1996 MKSS formed National Council for People's Right to Information in Delhi to raise RTI to the status of a national campaign.
- Prior to that, the Consumer Education and Research Center, the Press Council and the Shourie committee had proposed a draft RTI law.
- In 2002, a weak Freedom of Information Act was legislated but never came into force.
- In 2004 RTI Bill was tabled and received presidential assent in June 2005.

Exercise

1. Chipko movement was started in which of the following regions
   - (a) Uttarakhand
   - (b) Himachal Pradesh
   - (c) Punjab
   - (d) Uttar Pradesh

2. The Chipko movement, which started over a single issue, became a symbol of many such popular movements emerging in different parts of the country during the __________ and later.
   - (a) 1970's
   - (b) 1980's
   - (c) 1990's
   - (d) None of the following

3. Which of the following is the example of Party based movements
   - (a) Nationalist movement
   - (b) Anti-caste movement
   - (c) Kisan Sabhas
   - (d) Both (a) and (b)

4. Consider the following statements

   "In the 1970s and 1980s, many of the politically active groups lost faith in existing democratic institutions and electoral politics and therefore chose to step outside of party politics and engage in mass mobilisation for registering their protests."

   The above statement best describes which of the following movements
   - (a) Non-party movements
   - (b) Nationalist movement
   - (c) Democratic Movement
   - (d) None of the following

5. Dalit Panthers, a militant organisation of the Dalit youth, was formed in which of the following regions?
   - (a) Maharashtra
   - (b) Rajasthan
   - (c) Uttar Pradesh
   - (d) Gujrat

6. A comprehensive law to provided rigorous punishment for doing atrocities on Dalits in which of the following years?
   - (a) 1989
   - (b) 1990
   - (c) 1992
   - (d) 1991

7. Bharatiya Kisan Union (BKU), is an organisation of farmers from ______________ and ______________
   - (a) Haryana and Western Uttar Pradesh
   - (b) Eastern Uttar Pradesh and Punjab
   - (c) Haryana and Punjab
   - (d) Bihar and Uttar Pradesh

8. Find the incorrect statements with reference to the Bharatiya Kisan Union (BKU)
   - (a) The BKU was one of the leading organisations in the farmers' movement of the nineties
   - (b) Most of the BKU members belonged to a single community
   - (c) The BKU distanced itself from all political parties.
   - (d) It operated as a pressure group in politics with its strength of sheer numbers.

9. Shetkari Sanghatana of ______________ and Rayata Sangha of ____________ -, are some of the prominent examples of farmers organisations across states
   - (a) Gujrat, Kerala
   - (b) Maharashtra , Karnataka
   - (c) Uttar Pradesh and Gujrat
   - (d) None of the above

10. In which of the following states the anti-Arak movement took place?
    - (a) Andhra Pradesh
    - (b) Karnataka
    - (c) Kerala
    - (d) Rajasthan

11. In Anti-Arrack Movement, Rural women in remote villages from the State of Andhra Pradesh fought a battle against
    - (a) alcoholism
    - (b) a mafias
    - (c) the government
    - (d) All of the above

12. Consider the following statements
    1. Anti-arrack movement was a spontaneous mobilisation of women demanding a ban on the sale of alcohol in their neighbourhoods
    2. Gradually this anti-arrack movement touched upon larger social, economic and political issues of the region that affected women's life.
    3. As a result the movement made demands of equal representation to women in politics during the nineties.

    Choose the correct answer from the codes given below
    - (a) 1 and 3 only
    - (b) 2 and 3 only
    - (c) 1 and 2 only
    - (d) all of the above

13. Narmada and its tributaries flow across the states of
1. Madhya Pradesh
2. Gujarat
3. Maharashtra.
4. Rajasthan

Choose the correct answer from the codes given below
(a) 1 2 and 4 only
(b) 2 and 3 only
(c) 1 2 and 3 only
(d) all of the above

14. Sardar Sarovar Project in _____________and the Narmada Sagar Project in _____________were two of the most important and biggest, multi-purpose dams developmental project
(a) Gujrat , Madhya Pradesh
(b) Madhya Pradesh , Rajasthan
(c) Rajasthan , Madhya Pradesh
(d) Rajasthan, Gujrat

15. Consider the following statements about Narmada Bachao Aandolan
1. It opposed the construction of dams under Sardar Sarovar Project and the Narmada Sagar Project
2. The movement demanded proper rehabilitation of all those who were directly or indirectly affected by the project
3. The Supreme Court upheld the government's decision to go ahead with the construction of the dam

Choose the correct answer from the codes given below
(a) 1 and 3 only   (b) 2 and 3 only
(c) 1 and 2 only   (d) all of the above

16. Mazdoor Kisan Shakti Sangathan (MKSS) organisation was related to which of the following movements?
(a) Right to Information
(b) Equal representation to women in politics
(c) Panchayat reforms
(d) Lokpal

Answer Keys

1. (a)   2. (a)   3. (a)   4. (a)   5. (a)   6. (a)   7. (a)   8. (a)   9. (b)   10. (a)

11. (d)   12. (d)   13. (c)   14. (a)   15. (d)   16. (a)

Solutions

1. a

2. a

3. a
- Popular movements may take the form of social movements or political movements
- Example of Political movement - nationalist movement
- Example of Social movements - the anti-caste movement, the kisan sabhas and the trade union movement in early twentieth century.

4. a
- In the 1970s and 1980s, many sections of the society became disillusioned with the functioning of political parties.
- They therefore chose to step outside of party politics and engage in mass mobilisation for registering their protests.
- Because of the voluntary nature of their social work, many of these organisations came to be known as voluntary organisations or voluntary sector organisations.
- These voluntary organisations chose to remain outside party politics.
- They did not contest elections at the local or regional level nor did they support any one political party.
- These organisations were called 'non-party political formations'.

5. a
- Dalit Panthers, a militant organisation of the Dalit youth, was formed in Maharashtra in 1972

6. a

7. a

8. a
- Like the BKU, farmers' organisations across States recruited their members from communities that dominated regional electoral politics.

9. b

10. a

11. d

12. d

13. c

14. a

15. d
- Sardar Sarovar Project in Gujarat and the Narmada Sagar Project in Madhya Pradesh were two of the most important and biggest, multi-purpose dams planned under the project
- Narmada Bachao Aandolan, a movement to save Narmada , opposed the construction of these dams
- The movement demanded proper and just rehabilitation of all those who were directly or indirectly affected by the project.
- The Supreme Court upheld the government's decision to go ahead with the construction of the dam while also instructing to ensure proper rehabilitation.

16. a

CHAPTER 8

Regional Aspirations

1. Region and the Nation

- Indian approach to diversity – the Indian nation shall not deny the rights of different regions and linguistic groups to retain their own culture.
- Indian nationalism sought to balance the principles of unity and diversity.
- The Indian approach was very different from the one adopted in many European countries where they saw cultural diversity as a threat to the nation.
- India adopted a democratic approach to the question of diversity.
- Democracy allows the political expressions of regional aspirations
- Democratic politics allows parties and groups to address the people on the basis of their regional identity, aspiration and specific regional problems.
- Such an arrangement may sometimes lead to tensions and problems.
- Sometimes, the concern for national unity may overshadow the regional needs and aspirations.
- At other times a concern for region alone may blind us to the larger needs of the nation.

Areas of tension

- The issue of Jammu and Kashmir - It was a question of the political aspirations of the people of Kashmir valley.
- In some parts of the north-east, there was no consensus about being a part of India (eg. Nagaland and Mizoram)
- In the south, some groups from the Dravid movement briefly toyed with the idea of a separate country.
- Today's Andhra Pradesh, Karnataka, Maharashtra, and Gujarat were among the regions affected by mass agitations.

- There were protests against making Hindi the official national language of the country(in Tamil Nadu)
- In the north, there were strong pro-Hindi agitations demanding that Hindi be made the official language
- From the late 1950s, people speaking the Punjabi language started agitating for a separate State for themselves.
- This demand was finally accepted and the States of Punjab and Haryana were created in 1966.
- Later, the States of Chhattisgarh, Uttarakhand and Jharkhand were created.
- Thus the challenge of diversity was met by redrawing the internal boundaries of the country.

2. Jammu and Kashmir

- Jammu and Kashmir had a special status under Article 370 of the Indian Constitution.
- Jammu and Kashmir comprises three social and political regions— Jammu, Kashmir and Ladakh.
- The Jammu region is a mix of foothills and plains.
- It is predominantly inhabited by the Hindus.
- The Kashmir region mainly comprises of the Kashmir valley.
- It is inhabited mostly by Kashmiri Muslims with the remaining being Hindus, Sikhs, Buddhists and others.
- The Ladakh region is mainly mountainous. It has very little population which is almost equally divided between Buddhists and Muslims.

Roots of the Problem

- Before 1947, Jammu and Kashmir (J&K) was a Princely State under the rule of. Maharaja Hari Singh
- The ruler of Kashmir, Maharaja Hari Singh did not want to merge either with India or Pakistan but to have an independent status for his state.

- In October 1947, Pakistan sent tribal infiltrators from its side to capture Kashmir.
- This forced the Maharaja to ask for Indian military help.
- India extended the military support and drove back the infiltrators from Kashmir valley, but only after the Maharaja had signed an 'Instrument of Accession' with the Government of India.
- The issue was taken to the Union Nations Organisation, which in its resolution dated 21 April 1948 recommended a three step process to resolve the issue.
- Firstly, Pakistan had to withdraw its entire nationalities, who entered into Kashmir.
- Secondly, India needed to progressively reduce its forces so as to maintain law and order. Thirdly, a plebiscite was to be conducted in a free and impartial manner.
- However, no progress could be achieved under this resolution.

Politics since 1948

Politics in India since Independence

- Sheikh Abdullah took over as the Prime Minister of the State of J&K in March 1948 while India agreed to grant it provisional autonomy under the Article 370.
- The head of the government in the State was then called Prime Minister.
- He was dismissed in 1953 by the Centre government and kept in detention for a number of years.
- A change in the provision of the Constitution of Jammu and Kashmir was made in 1965 by which the Prime Minister of the state was designated as Chief Minister of the state.
- Accordingly, Ghulam Mohammed Sadiq of the Indian National Congress became the first Chief Minister of the state.
- In 1974 Sheikh Abdullah became the Chief Minister of the State.
- Sheikh Abdullah died in 1982 and the leadership of the National Conference went to his son, Farooq Abdullah, who became the Chief Minister.

Insurgency and After

- By 1989, the State had come in the grip of a militant movement mobilised around the cause of a separate Kashmiri nation.
- The insurgents got moral, material and military support from Pakistan.

- For a number of years the State was under President's rule and effectively under the control of the armed forces.
- Throughout the period from 1990, Jammu and Kashmir experienced extraordinary violence at the hands of the insurgents and through army action.
- Assembly elections were held in 1996 in which the National Conference led by Farooq Abdullah came to power with a demand for regional autonomy for Jammu and Kashmir.
- At the end of its term, elections were held in the State in 2002.
- The National Conference failed to win a majority and was replaced by a coalition government of People's Democratic Party (PDP) and Congress.

2002 and Beyond

- President rule was imposed in the state in July 2008.
- The next election was held in November-December 2008.
- Another coalition government (composed of NC and INC) came into power headed by Omar Abdullah in 2009.
- In 2014, the state went into another election, which recorded the highest voters' turnout in 25 years.
- A coalition government led by Mufti Mohammed Sayeed of the PDP came into power with the BJP as its partner.
- After Mufti Mohammed Sayeed died, his daughter Mahbooba Mufti became the first woman Chief Minister of the state in April 2016.
- The President's rule was imposed in June 2018 after BJP withdrew its support to the Mufti government.
- On 5 August 2019, Article 370 was abolished by the Jammu & Kashmir Reorganisation Act 2019 and the state was constituted into two Union Territories, viz., Jammu & Kashmir and Ladakh.

3. Punjab

- The decade of 1980s also witnessed major developments in the State of Punjab.
- The social composition of the State changed first with Partition and later on after the carving out of Haryana and Himachal Pradesh.
- While the rest of the country was reorganised on linguistic lines in 1950s, Punjab had to wait till 1966 for the creation of a Punjabi speaking State.

- The Akali Dal, which was formed in 1920 as the political wing of the Sikhs, had led the movement for the formation of a 'Punjabi suba'.

Political context

- After the reorganisation, the Akalis came to power in 1967 and then in 1977.
- On both the occasions it was a coalition government.
- During the 1970s a section of Akalis began to demand political autonomy for the region.
- The Anandpur Sahib Resolution(1973) passed by the Akalis asserted regional autonomy and wanted to redefine centre-state relationship in the country.
- The Resolution was a plea for strengthening federalism, but it could also be interpreted as a plea for a separate Sikh nation.
- The Akali government got dismissed in 1980
- After that , the Akali Dal launched a movement on the question of the distribution of water between Punjab and its neighbouring States.

Cycle of violence

- Soon, the leadership of the movement passed from the moderate Akalis to the extremist elements and took the form of armed insurgency.
- These militants made their headquarters inside the Sikh holy shrine, the Golden Temple in Amritsar, and turned it into an armed fortress.
- In June 1984, the Government of India carried out 'Operation Blue Star', code name for army action in the Golden Temple.
- In this operation, the Government could successfully flush out the militants, but it also damaged the historic temple and deeply hurt the sentiments of the Sikhs.
- This military operation gave further impetus to militant and extremist groups.
- Prime Minister Indira Gandhi was assassinated on 31 October 1984 outside her residence by her bodyguards.
- Both the assassins were Sikhs and wanted to take revenge for Operation Bluestar.
- In Delhi and in many parts of northern India violence broke out against the Sikh community. The violence against the Sikhs continued for almost a week.

Road to Peace

- In 1984, the new Prime Minister Rajiv Gandhi initiated a dialogue with moderate Akali leaders.

- In July 1985, he reached an agreement with Harchand Singh Longowal, then the President of the Akali Dal.
- This agreement, known as the Rajiv Gandhi - Longowal Accord or the Punjab Accord, was a step towards bringing normalcy to Punjab.
- It was agreed that Chandigarh would be transferred to Punjab, a separate commission would be appointed to resolve the border dispute between Punjab and Haryana, and a tribunal would be set up to decide the sharing of Ravi-Beas river water among Punjab, Haryana and Rajasthan.
- The agreement also provided for compensation to and better treatment of those affected by the militancy in Punjab and the withdrawal of the application of Armed Forces Special Powers Act in Punjab.
- However, peace did not come easily or immediately. The cycle of violence continued nearly for a decade.
- Militancy was eventually eradicated by the security forces. But the losses incurred by the people of Punjab – Sikhs and Hindus alike – were enormous.
- Peace returned to Punjab by the middle of 1990s
- The alliance of Akali Dal (Badal) and the BJP scored a major victory in1997, in the first normal elections in the State in the post-militancy era.

4. North -East

- In the North-East, regional aspirations reached a turning point in 1980s.
- This region now consists of seven States, also referred to as the 'seven sisters'.
- The region has only 4 per cent of the country's population but about twice as much share of its area.
- A small corridor of about 22 kilometers connects the region to the rest of the country. Otherwise the region shares boundaries with China, Myanmar and Bangladesh and serves as India's gateway to South East Asia.
- Tripura, Manipur and Khasi Hills of Meghalaya were erstwhile Princely States which merged with India after Independence.
- Nagaland State was created in 1963; Manipur, Tripura and Meghalaya in 1972 while Mizoram and Arunachal Pradesh became separate States only in 1987.
- The Partition of India in 1947 had reduced the North-East to a land locked region and affected its economy.

- Cut off from the rest of India, the region suffered neglect in developmental terms.
- The vast international border and weak communication between the North-East and the rest of India have further added to the delicate nature of politics there.
- Three issues dominate the politics of North-East: demands for autonomy, movements for secession, and opposition to 'outsiders'.
- Major initiatives on the first issue in the 1970s set the stage for some dramatic developments on the second and the third in the 1980s.

Demands for autonomy

- At independence the entire region except Manipur and Tripura comprised the State of Assam.
- Demands for political autonomy arose when the non-Assamese felt that the Assam government
- The Central Government had to create Meghalaya, Mizoram and Arunachal Pradesh out of Assam.
- Tripura and Manipur were upgraded into States too.
- The reorganisation of the North-East was completed by 1972.
- But this was not the end of autonomy demands in this region.
- In Assam, for example, communities like the Bodos, Karbis and Dimasas wanted separate States.
- Karbis and Dimasas have been granted autonomy under District Councils while Bodos were recently granted Autonomous Council.

Secessionist movements (Mizoram and Nagaland)

- After Independence, the Mizo Hills area was made an autonomous district within Assam.
- Some Mizos believed that they were never a part of British India and therefore did not belong to the Indian union.
- But the movement for secession gained popular support after the Assam government failed to respond adequately to the great famine of 1959 in Mizo hills.
- The Mizos' anger led to the formation of the Mizo National Front (MNF) under the leadership of Laldenga.
- In 1966 the MNF started an armed campaign for independence.

- Thus, started a two decade long battle between Mizo insurgents and the Indian army.
- The MNF fought a guerilla war, got support from Pakistani government and secured shelter in the then East Pakistan.
- The Indian security forces countered it with a series of repressive measures
- At the end of two decades of insurgency everyone was a loser.
- Laldenga came back from exile in Pakistan and started negotiations with the Indian government.
- Rajiv Gandhi steered these negotiations to a positive conclusion.
- In 1986 a peace agreement was signed between Rajiv Gandhi and Laldenga.
- As per this accord Mizoram was granted full-fledged statehood with special powers and the MNF agreed to give up secessionist struggle.
- Laldenga took over as the Chief Minister.
- The story of Nagaland is similar to Mizoram, except that it started much earlier and has not yet had such a happy ending.
- Led by Angami Zaphu Phizo, a section of the Nagas declared independence from India way back in 1951.
- Phizo turned down many offers of negotiated settlement.
- The Naga National Council launched an armed struggle for sovereignty of Nagas.
- After a period of violent insurgency a section of the Nagas signed an agreement with the Government of India but this was not acceptable to other rebels.
- The problem in Nagaland still awaits a final resolution.

5. Movements against outsiders

- The Assam Movement from 1979 to 1985 is the best example of movements against 'outsiders'. The Assamese suspected that there were huge numbers of illegal Bengali Muslim settlers from Bangladesh.
- They felt that unless these foreign nationals are detected and deported they would reduce the indigenous Assamese into a minority.
- In 1979 the All Assam Students' Union (AASU), a students' group not affiliated to any party, led an anti-foreigner movement.
- The movement was against illegal migrations, against domination of Bengalis and other

- outsiders, and against faulty voters' register that included the names of lakhs of immigrants.
- The movement demanded that all outsiders who had entered the State after 1951 should be sent back.
- Eventually after six years of turmoil, the Rajiv Gandhi-led government entered into negotiations with the AASU leaders, leading to the signing of an accord in 1985.
- According to this agreement those foreigners who migrated into Assam during and after Bangladesh war and since, were to be identified and deported.
- Assam accord brought peace and changed the face of politics in Assam, but it did not solve the problem of immigration.
- The issue of the 'outsiders' continues to be a live issue in the politics of Assam and many other places in the North-East.

6. Goa's liberation

- Although the British empire in India came to an end in 1947, Portugal refused to withdraw from the territories of Goa, Diu and Daman which were under its colonial rule since the sixteenth century.
- During their long rule, the Portuguese suppressed the people of Goa, denied them civil rights, and carried out forced religious conversions.
- After India's Independence, the Indian government tried very patiently to persuade the Portuguese government to withdraw.
- Finally, in December 1961, the Government of India sent the army which liberated these territories after barely two days of action. Goa, Diu and Daman became Union Territory.
- In January 1967, the Central Government held a special 'opinion poll' in Goa asking people to decide if they wanted to be part of Maharashtra or remain separate.
- A referendum-like procedure was used to ascertain people's wishes on this issue.
- The majority voted in favour of remaining outside of Maharashtra.
- Thus, Goa continued as a Union Territory.
- Finally, in 1987, Goa became a State of the Indian Union.

Exercise

1. Consider the following statements with reference to the Indian approach to diversity
   1. The Indian approach was very similar from the one adopted in many European countries
   2. European countries saw cultural diversity as a threat to the nation.

   Choose the correct answer from the codes given below
   - (a) 1 only
   - (b) 2 only
   - (c) both 1 and 2
   - (d) Neither 1 nor 2

2. Consider the following statements about Democracy
   1. Democracy allows the political expressions of regional aspirations
   2. Democratic politics allows parties and groups to address the people on the basis of their regional identity and specific regional problems

   Choose the correct answer from the codes given below
   - (a) 1 only
   - (b) 2 only
   - (c) both 1 and 2
   - (d) Neither 1 nor 2

3. The States of Punjab and Haryana were created in
   - (a) 1966
   - (b) 1968
   - (c) 1971
   - (d) 1972

4. Which of the following states were created after the creation of Punjab and Haryana states?
   - (a) Chhattisgarh
   - (b) Uttarakhand
   - (c) Jharkhand
   - (d) All of the above

5. Find the incorrect statement about Jammu and Kashmir
   - (a) Jammu region is predominantly inhabited by the Hindus.
   - (b) Kashmir region mainly comprises of the Kashmir valley.
   - (c) Kashmir region is inhabited mostly by Kashmiri Muslims
   - (d) The Jammu region mainly comprises of plains only

6. Before 1947, Jammu and Kashmir (J&K) was a Princely State under the rule of
   - (a) Maharaj Ranjeet Singh
   - (b) Maharaja Hari Singh
   - (c) Maharaj Amarjit Dev
   - (d) None of the above

7. The Maharaja of Jammu and Kashmir had signed an 'Instrument of Accession' with which of the following nations?
   - (a) India
   - (b) Pakistan
   - (c) United Nations
   - (d) Both a and b

8. The India- Pakistan issue was taken to the Union Nations Organisation, which in its resolution dated 21 April 1948 recommended which of the following process to resolve the issue.
   - (a) Pakistan had to withdraw its entire nationalities, who entered into Kashmir.
   - (b) India needed to progressively reduce its forces so as to maintain law and order.
   - (c) A plebiscite was to be conducted in a free and impartial manner.
   - (d) All of the above

9. Find the true statement with reference to the Politics of J&K after independence
   - (a) Sheikh Abdullah took over as the Chief Minister of the State of J&K in March 1948
   - (b) India agreed to grant it complete autonomy under the Article 370.
   - (c) The head of the government in the State was then called Prime Minister.
   - (d) A change in the provision of the Constitution of Jammu and Kashmir was made in 1965

10. In which of the following year elections were held in the state of J&K
    - (a) 1996
    - (b) 2002
    - (c) 2008
    - (d) All of the above

11. Who became the first woman Chief Minister of the state of J&K
    - (a) Mahbooba Mufti
    - (b) Mohammed Sayeed
    - (c) Kazri Begum
    - (d) None of the above

12. On 5 August 2019, Article 370 was abolished by the Jammu & Kashmir Reorganisation Act 2019 and the state was constituted into two Union Territories i.e. ________ and ________
    - (a) Jammu and Kashmir
    - (b) Jammu Kashmir and Ladakh
    - (c) Kashmir and Ladakh
    - (d) None of the above

13. The social composition of the Punjab State changed first with Partition and later on after the carving out of ______and ______

(a) Haryana and Himachal Pradesh.

(b) Himachal Pradesh and Delhi

(c) Haryana and Delhi

(d) Rajasthan and Haryana

14. The Anandpur Sahib Resolution(1973) was passed by which of the following organisations?

(a) Punjab government

(b) Centre Government

(c) Sikh committee

(d) Golden temple (SGPC)

15. The Government of India carried out 'Operation Blue Star', code name for army action in the Golden Temple in which of the following years?

(a) 1984　　　　(b) 1988

(c) 1982　　　　(d) 1982

16. Punjab Accord was signed between

(a) Longowal and Rajeev Gandhi

(b) I.K Gujral and Akalidal

(c) Indira Gandhi and Longowal

(d) Punjab and Haryana

17. Find the incorrect pair

State	Created in
(a) Nagaland	1963
(b) Manipur	1972
(c) Tripura	1987
(d) Meghalaya	1972

18. Which of the following states were created out of assam

1. Meghalaya
2. Mizoram
3. Arunachal Pradesh
4. Tripura

Choose the correct answer from the codes given below

(a) 1 and 3 only　　　(b) 1 2 and 3 only

(c) 1 and 2 only　　　(d) 1 2 3 and 4

19. Bodos, Karbis and Dimasas communities were present in which of the following states?

(a) Assam　　　　(b) Tripura

(c) Manipur　　　(d) Meghalaya

20. Goa became a State of the Indian Union in ______

(a) 1987　　　　(b) 1961

(c) 1947　　　　(d) 1966

Answer Keys

1. (b)	2. (c)	3. (a)	4. (d)	5. (d)	6. (b)	7. (a)	8. (d)	9. (d)	10. (d)
11. (a)	12. (b)	13. (a)	14. (a)	15. (a)	16. (a)	17. (c)	18. (b)	19. (a)	20. (a)

Solutions

1. b
- The Indian approach was very different from the one adopted in many European countries where they saw cultural diversity as a threat to the nation.
- India adopted a democratic approach to the question of diversity.

2. c

3. a

4. d

5. d

6. b
- Before 1947, Jammu and Kashmir (J&K) was a Princely State under the rule of. Maharaja Hari Singh

7. a
- The ruler of Kashmir, Maharaja Hari Singh did not want to merge either with India or Pakistan but to have an independent status for his state.

8. d
- However, no progress could be achieved under this resolution.

9. d

10. d
- Throughout the period from 1990, Jammu and Kashmir experienced extraordinary violence at the hands of the insurgents and through army action.
- Assembly elections were held in 1996 in which the National Conference led by Farooq Abdullah came to power with a demand for regional autonomy for Jammu and Kashmir.
- At the end of its term, elections were held in the State in 2002.
- The National Conference failed to win a majority and was replaced by a coalition government of People's Democratic Party (PDP) and Congress.
- President rule was imposed in the state in July 2008.
- The next election was held in November-December 2008.

11. a

12. b

13. a

14. a
- After the reorganisation, the Akalis came to power in 1967 and then in 1977.
- During the 1970s a section of Akalis began to demand political autonomy for the region.
- The Anandpur Sahib Resolution(1973) passed by the Akalis asserted regional autonomy and wanted to redefine centre-state relationship in the country.

15. a
- In June 1984, the Government of India carried out 'Operation Blue Star', code name for army action in the Golden Temple.

16. a
- In 1984, the new Prime Minister Rajiv Gandhi initiated a dialogue with moderate Akali leaders.
- In July 1985, he reached an agreement with Harchand Singh Longowal, then the President of the Akali Dal.
- This agreement, known as the Rajiv Gandhi - Longowal Accord or the Punjab Accord, was a step towards bringing normalcy to Punjab.

17. c

18. b
- At independence the entire region except Manipur and Tripura comprised the State of Assam.
- The Central Government had to create Meghalaya, Mizoram and Arunachal Pradesh out of Assam.

19. a

20. a

CHAPTER 9

Recent Developments in Indian Politics Context of the 1990s

Developments

1.
   - Rajiv Gandhi became the Prime Minister after the assassination of Indira Gandhi.
   - Congress won the Lok Sabha elections held immediately thereafter in 1984.
   - Congress party got defeated in the elections held in 1989.
   - The Congress came back to power after the mid-term elections held in 1991.
   - The elections of 1989 marked the end of what political scientists have called the 'Congress system'.

2.
   - Another development was the rise of the 'Mandal issue' in national politics.
   - Recommendation of Mandal Commission - jobs in central government should be reserved for the Other Backward Classes.
   - The dispute between the supporters and opponents of OBC reservations was known as the 'Mandal issue' and was to play an important role in shaping politics since 1989.

3.
   - The new economic reforms first became very visible in 1991 and radically changed the direction that the Indian economy had pursued since Independence.
   - These policies have been widely criticised by various movements and organisations. But the various governments that came to power in this period have continued to follow these.

4.
   - A number of events culminated in the demolition of the disputed structure at Ayodhya (known as Babri Masjid) in December 1992.
   - This event symbolised and triggered various changes in the politics of the country and intensified debates about the nature of Indian nationalism and secularism.
   - These developments are associated with the rise of the BJP and the politics of 'Hindutva'.

Assassination of Rajiv Gandhi

- The assassination of Rajiv Gandhi in May 1991 led to a change in leadership of the Congress party.
- He was assassinated by a Sri Lankan Tamil linked to the LTTE when he was on an election campaign tour in Tamil Nadu.
- In the elections of 1991, Congress emerged as the single largest party.
- Following Rajiv Gandhi's death, the party chose Narsimha Rao as the Prime Minister.

Era of Coalitions

- Elections in 1989 - Congress was the largest party in the Lok Sabha but it did not have a clear majority
- The National Front (which itself was an alliance of Janata Dal and some other regional parties) received support from two diametrically opposite political groups: the BJP and the Left Front.
- On this basis, the National Front formed a coalition government, but the BJP and the Left Front did not join in this government.

What happened after 1989

- Emergence of several parties in such a way that one or two parties did not get most of the votes or seats.

- This also meant that no single party secured a clear majority of seats in any Lok Sabha election held since 1989 till 2014.
- This development initiated an era of coalition governments at the Centre, in which regional parties played a crucial role in forming ruling alliances.

Alliance politics

- The nineties also saw the emergence of powerful regional parties
- These parties played an important role in the United Front government that came to power in 1996.
- The United Front was similar to the National Front of 1989 for it included Janata Dal and several regional parties.
- This time the BJP did not support the government. The United Front government was supported by the Congress.
- In 1989, both the Left and the BJP supported the National Front Government because they wanted to keep the Congress out of power.
- In 1996, the Left continued to support the non-Congress government but this time the Congress, supported it, as both the Congress and the Left wanted to keep the BJP out of power.
- BJP emerged as the largest party in the 1996 election but could not secure a majority in the Lok Sabha.
- It finally came to power by leading It finally came to power by leading a coalition government from May 1998 to June 1999 and was re-elected in October 1999.
- Atal Behari Vajpayee was the Prime Minister during both these NDA governments and his government formed in 1999 completed its full term.
- Thus, with the elections of 1989, a long phase of coalition politics began in India.

Government formed with the participation or support of many regional parties.

1. National Front in 1989
2. United Front in 1996 and 1997
3. NDA in 1997
4. BJP-led coalition in 1998
5. NDA in 1999
6. UPA in 2004 and 2009.

This trend changed in 2014.

Political Rise of Other Backward Classes

- One long-term development of this period was the rise of backward Classes as a political force.

- OBC - These are communities other than SC and ST
- The rise of these parties first found political expression at the national level in the form of the Janata Party government in 1977.
- The decision of the National Front government to implement the recommendations of the Mandal Commission further helped in shaping the politics of 'Other Backward Classes'.
- In 1978 the Backward and Minority Communities Employees Federation (BAMCEF) was formed.
- It took a strong position in favour of political power to the 'bahujan' – the SC, ST, OBC and minorities.
- It was out of this that the subsequent Dalit Shoshit Samaj Sangharsh Samiti and later the Bahujan Samaj Party (BSP) emerged under the leadership of Kanshi Ram.
- The BSP began as a small party supported largely by Dalit voters in Punjab, Haryana and Uttar Pradesh.
- But in 1989 and the 1991 elections, it achieved a breakthrough in Uttar Pradesh.
- This was the first time in independent India that a political party supported mainly by Dalit voters had achieved this kind of political success.

The Mandal Commission

- Reservations for the OBC were in existence in southern States since the 1960s
- But this policy was not operative in north Indian States.
- During the tenure of Janata Party government in 1977-79, the demand for reservations for backward castes in north India and at the national level was strongly raised.
- The central government appointed a Commission in 1978 to look into and recommend ways to improve the conditions of the backward classes.
- This was the second time since Independence that the government had appointed such a commission.
- Therefore, this commission was officially known as the Second Backward Classes Commission.
- Popularly, the commission is known as the Mandal Commission, after the name of its Chairperson, Bindeshwari Prasad Mandal.
- The Commission gave its recommendations in 1980. By then the Janata government had fallen.
- The Commission recommended reserving 27 per cent of seats in educational institutions and government jobs for these groups.

- The Mandal Commission also made many other recommendations, like, land reform, to improve the conditions of the OBCs.
- In August 1990, the National Front government decided to implement one of the recommendations of Mandal Commission
- This decision sparked agitations and violent protests in many cities of north India.
- The decision was also challenged in the Supreme Court and came to be known as the 'Indira Sawhney case', after the name of one of the petitioners.
- In November 1992, the Supreme Court gave a ruling upholding the decision of the government.

Communalism, Secularism, Democracy

- The other long-term development during this period was the rise of politics based on religious identity
- After the fall of the Janata Party and its break-up, the supporters of erstwhile Jana Sangh formed the Bharatiya Janata Party (BJP) in 1980.
- The BJP pursued the politics of 'Hindutva' and adopted the strategy of mobilising the Hindus.
- Hindutva literally means 'Hinduness' and was defined by its originator, V. D. Savarkar, as the basis of Indian (in his language also Hindu) nationhood.
- It basically meant that to be members of the Indian nation, everyone must not only accept India as their 'fatherland' (*pitrubhu*) but also as their holy land (*punyabhu*).
- Two developments around 1986 became central to the politics of BJP as a 'Hindutva' party.

The first was the Shah Bano case in 1985.

- In this case a 62-year old divorced Muslim woman, had filed a case for maintenance from her former husband.
- The Supreme Court ruled in her favour.
- The orthodox Muslims saw the Supreme Court's order as an interference in Muslim Personal Law.
- On the demand of some Muslim leaders, the government passed the Muslim Women (Protection of Rights on Divorce) Act, 1986 that nullified the Supreme Court's judgment.
- This action of the government was opposed by many women's organisations, many Muslim groups and most of the intellectuals.
- The BJP criticised this action of the Congress government as an unnecessary concession and 'appeasement' of the minority community.

The second was the ***Ayodhya dispute***

- The second development was the order by the Faizabad district court in February 1986.
- The court ordered that the Babri Masjid premises be unlocked so that Hindus could offer prayers at the site which they considered as a temple.
- A dispute had been going on for many decades over the mosque known as Babri Masjid at Ayodhya.
- The Babri Masjid was a 16th century mosque in Ayodhya and was built by Mir Baqi – Mughal emperor Babur's General.
- Some Hindus believe that it was built after demolishing a temple for Lord Rama in what is believed to be his birthplace.
- The dispute took the form of a court case and has continued for many decades.
- In the late 1940s the mosque was locked up as the matter was with the court.
- As soon as the locks of the Babri Masjid were opened, mobilisation began on both sides.
- This large scale mobilisation led to surcharged atmosphere and many instances of communal violence
- The BJP made this issue its major electoral and political plank.
- The BJP, in order to generate public support, took out a massive march called the *Rathyatra* from Somnath in Gujarat to Ayodhya in UP.

Demolition and after

- Thousands of people gathered from all over the country at Ayodhya on 6 December 1992 and demolished the mosque.
- This news led to clashes between the Hindus and Muslims in many parts of the country.

Gujarat riots

- In February-March 2002, large-scale violence took place in Gujarat.
- The immediate provocation for this violence was an incident that took place at a station called Godhra.
- A bogey of a train that was returning from Ayodhya and was full of *Karsevaks* was set on fire. Fifty- seven people died in that fire.
- Suspecting the hand of the Muslims in setting fire to the bogey, large-scale violence against Muslims began in many parts of Gujarat from the next day.
- This violence continued for almost a whole month. Nearly 1100 persons, mostly Muslims, were killed in this violence.

Lok Sabha Elections 2004

- The NDA was defeated and a new coalition government led by the Congress, known as the United Progressive Alliance came to power.

- The party system has now changed almost dramatically from what it was till the seventies.

- The situation suggests that political competition will be multi-cornered.

- By implication the situation also assumes a divergence of political ideologies.

- However, on many crucial issues, a broad agreement has emerged among most parties.

- In the midst of severe competition and many conflicts, a consensus appears to have emerged among most parties.

This consensus consists of four elements.

1. Agreement on new economic policies

2. Acceptance of the political and social claims of the backward castes

3. Acceptance of the role of State level parties in governance of the country

4. Emphasis on pragmatic considerations rather than ideological positions and political alliances without ideological agreement

- Coalition politics has shifted the focus of political parties from ideological differences to power sharing arrangements.

- Thus, most parties of the NDA did not agree with the 'Hindutva' ideology of the BJP.

- Yet, they came together to form a government and remained in power for a full term.

Exercise

1. Find the correct statement with reference to the Developments in Indian politics in the context of 1990s

    (a) Indra Kumar Gujral became the Prime Minister after the assassination of Indira Gandhi.

    (b) Congress won the Lok Sabha elections of 1984

    (c) Congress party also won the elections of 1989.

    (d) The Congress party lost the mid-term elections held in 1991.

2. Which of the following Lok Sabha elections marked the end of the Congress system

    (a) Elections of 1991

    (b) Elections of 1984

    (c) Elections of 1989

    (d) None of the above

3. Which of the following events is/are the major political developments of 1990's

    (a) Mandal Commission

    (b) New economic reforms

    (c) Babri Masjid demolition

    (d) all of the above

4. Which of the following events radically changed the direction that the Indian economy had pursued since Independence?

    (a) New economic reforms

    (b) Banking Privatization

    (c) Banking Regulation act

    (d) Sensex

5. Following Rajiv Gandhi's death, the congress party chose ___________ as the Prime Minister

    (a) Narsimha Rao   (b) I.K Gujral

    (c) H.D Devegoda   (d) None of the above

6. Rajiv Gandhi was assassinated by which of the following terror organisations?

    (a) LTTE

    (b) Sri Lankan Tamil

    (c) Sri Lankan Rebels

    (d) Tamil Liberation Army

7. Consider the following statements about the Election of 1989

    1. The Janta Party formed a coalition government

    2. Congress was the largest party in the Lok Sabha

    Choose the true statement from the options given below

    (a) 1 only   (b) 2 only

    (c) Both 1 and 2   (d) Neither 1 nor 2

8. National Front was an alliance of ________ and some other regional parties

    (a) BJP   (b) Janata Dal

    (c) Left front   (d) None of the above

9. United Front government that came to power in ______

   (a) 1996   (b) 1998
   (c) 2004   (d) 1986

10. Consider the following statements about the election of 1996
    1. United Front government came to power in 1996.
    2. United Front was similar to the National Front of 1989
    3. BJP supported the United Front government

    Choose the true statement from the options given below
    (a) 1 and 2 only   (b) 2 only
    (c) 1 and 3 only   (d) All of the above

11. Find the incorrect statement with reference to. the Alliance politics of 1980's and 1990's
    (a) In 1989, both the Left and the BJP supported the National Front Government
    (b) In 1996, the Left support the non-Congress government
    (c) In 1989 and 1996, the BJP supported the government
    (d) None of the above

12. Find the true statement with reference to the formation of the BJP government in Centre
    (a) BJP emerged as the largest party in the 1996 election
    (b) BJP came to power by leading a coalition government in the 1996 elections
    (c) NDA government formed in 1999 completed its full term.
    (d) Both (a) and (c)

13. Which of the following government was formed *with the participation or support of many regional parties.*
    1. National Front   2. United Front
    3. NDA   4. UPA

    Choose the true statement from the options given below
    (a) 1 and 2 only   (b) 2 and 4 only
    (c) 1 and 3 only   (d) All of the above

14. The term Bahujan represents
    1. SC
    2. ST
    3. OBC
    4. Minorities

Choose the true statement from the options given below
(a) 1 and 2 only   (b) 2 and 4 only
(c) 1 and 3 only   (d) All of the above

15. Which of the following government decided to implement the recommendations of the Mandal Commission
    (a) National Front government
    (b) United Front government
    (c) NDA
    (d) BJP-led coalition

16. Backward and Minority Communities Employees Federation (BAMCEF) was formed in
    (a) 1977   (b) 1978
    (c) 1986   (d) 1988

17. Dalit Shoshit Samaj Sangharsh Samiti and later the Bahujan Samaj Party (BSP) emerged under the leadership of ________
    (a) Mayawati
    (b) Kanshi Ram.
    (c) Bindeshwari Prasad Mandal
    (d) None of the above

18. Find the incorrect statement with reference to Mandal Commission
    (a) It was appointed by the Janata Party government
    (b) This was the first time since Independence that the government had appointed such a commission.
    (c) The Commission recommended reserving 27 per cent of seats in educational institutions and government jobs for the OBCs
    (d) Both (a) and (c)

19. In August 1990, the National Front government decided to implement one of the recommendations of Mandal Commission. The decision was also challenged in the Supreme Court and came to be known as the ___________ after the name of one of the petitioners.
    (a) Indira Sawhney case
    (b) K.M. Nanavati vs State of Maharashtra
    (c) Kesavananda Bharti vs State of Kerala
    (d) Bhawal Case

20. The Babri Masjid was a 16th century mosque in Ayodhya built by
    (a) Mir Baqi   (b) Babur
    (c) Mir Badauni   (d) Mir Baksh

Answer Keys

1. (b)	2. (c)	3. (d)	4. (a)	5. (a)	6. (a)	7. (b)	8. (b)	9. (a)	10. (a)
11. (c)	12. (d)	13. (d)	14. (d)	15. (a)	16. (b)	17. (b)	18. (b)	19. (a)	20. (a)

Solutions

1. b
- Rajiv Gandhi became the Prime Minister after the assassination of Indira Gandhi.

2. c
- The elections of 1989 marked the end of what political scientists have called the 'Congress system'.

3. d

4. a

5. a

6. a
- Rajiv Gandhi was assassinated by a Sri Lankan Tamil linked to the LTTE when he was on an election campaign tour in Tamil Nadu.

7. b
- Elections in 1989 - Congress was the largest party in the Lok Sabha but it did not have a clear majority
- The National Front formed a coalition government, but the BJP and the Left Front did not join in this government.

8. b
- The National Front (which itself was an alliance of Janata Dal and some other regional parties) received support from two diametrically opposite political groups: the BJP and the Left Front.

9. a

10. a
- United Front government came to power in 1996.
- The United Front was similar to the National Front of 1989 for it included Janata Dal and several regional parties.
- BJP did not support the government. The United Front government was supported by the Congress.

11. c
- In 1989, both the Left and the BJP supported the National Front Government because they wanted to keep the Congress out of power.
- In 1996, the Left continued to support the non-Congress government but this time the Congress, supported it, as both the Congress and the Left wanted to keep the BJP out of power.

12. d
- BJP emerged as the largest party in the 1996 election but could not secure a majority in the Lok Sabha.
- It finally came to power by leading It finally came to power by leading a coalition government from May 1998 to June 1999 and was re-elected in October 1999.

13. d Government formed with the participation or support of many regional parties.
- National Front in 1989
- United Front in 1996 and 1997
- NDA in 1997
- BJP-led coalition in 1998
- NDA in 1999
- UPA in 2004 and 2009.

14. d

15. a
- The decision of the National Front government to implement the recommendations of the Mandal Commission further helped in shaping the politics of 'Other Backward Classes'.

16. b
- In 1978 the Backward and Minority Communities Employees Federation (BAMCEF) was formed.
- It took a strong position in favour of political power to the 'bahujan' – the SC, ST, OBC and minorities.

17. b

18. b
- The central government appointed a Commission in 1978 to look into and recommend ways to improve the conditions of the backward classes.
- This was the second time since Independence that the government had appointed such a commission.
- Therefore, this commission was officially known as the Second Backward Classes Commission.

19. a
- In August 1990, the National Front government decided to implement one of the recommendations of Mandal Commission
- This decision sparked agitations and violent protests in many cities of north India.
- The decision was also challenged in the Supreme Court and came to be known as the 'Indira Sawhney case', after the name of one of the petitioners.
- In November 1992, the Supreme Court gave a ruling upholding the decision of the government.

20. a

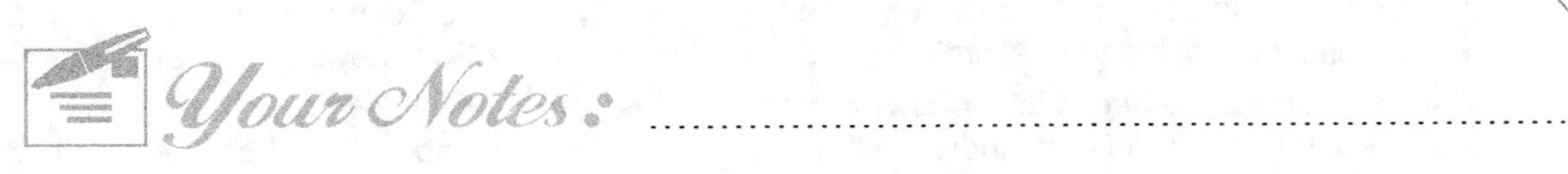

Your Notes :